THE

JEWELLER'S ASSISTANT

THE

JEWELLER'S ASSISTANT

IN

THE ART OF WORKING IN GOLD

A PRACTICAL TREATISE FOR MASTERS AND WORK-
MEN, COMPILED FROM THE EXPERIENCE OF
THIRTY YEARS' WORKSHOP PRACTICE

By GEORGE E. GEE

GOLDSMITH AND SILVERSMITH,

AUTHOR OF "THE GOLDSMITH'S HANDBOOK," "THE SILVERSMITH'S HANDBOOK,"
"THE HALL MARKING OF JEWELLERY," ETC., ETC.

Capio Lumen

LONDON
CROSBY LOCKWOOD AND SON
7, STATIONERS' HALL COURT, LUDGATE HILL
1892

PREFACE.

CONSIDERING the steady progress that has been made of late years, both in the mechanical and chemical departments of the jewellery trade, the necessity for an advanced work treating upon the subject has oftentimes been greatly felt.

The Author has, therefore, much pleasure in presenting to the trade and all other interested persons a thoroughly practical treatise on the subject. He does so with confidence, for the following reasons :—

Firstly, a real desire to supply that want; secondly, in consequence of having been consulted by most of the leading firms in the principal jewellery centres in England, and having also received communications from nearly every part of the civilised world seeking information such as is herein contained; and thirdly, the possession of an extensive knowledge of the subject, acquired during more than thirty years' active workshop practice in every department.

The work is not written for beginners and young students, but for the advanced workmen of every branch, as well as their employers, both of whom will be able to glean much from its pages with which they were probably not formerly acquainted.

Every endeavour has been made to make the work as reliable as possible, and from the Author's large practical experience and close attention to all the matters treated of, its genuineness in that direction can be thoroughly relied upon, as almost everything in the work has been put to the test by the Author himself. And he ventures therefore to hope that, considering the aim and scope of the work, it will meet a demand much felt, and be welcomed as containing original matter which will prove widely acceptable to the trade.

STANDARD WORKS,
58, TENBY STREET NORTH, BIRMINGHAM,
March, 1892.

CONTENTS.

CHAPTER I.

THE CHEMICAL AND PHYSICAL PROPERTIES OF GOLD.

CHAPTER II.

THE PRECIPITATION OF GOLD IN WASTE SOLUTION.

CHAPTER III.

THE DIFFERENT COLOURS OF GOLD.

CHAPTER IV.

THE MIXING AND MELTING OF GOLD.

b

CHAPTER V.

THE DRY-COLOURING OF GOLD.

CHAPTER VI.

THE WET-COLOURING OF GOLD.

CHAPTER VII.

THE MELTING AND CASTING OF GOLD.

CHAPTER VIII.

ELECTRO-GILDING.

CHAPTER IX.

SOME OTHER MODES OF GILDING.

CHAPTER X.

PRACTICAL MANIPULATIONS.

CHAPTER XI.

MIXING ALLOYS.

CHAPTER XIV.

COLLECTING AND REFINING.

CHAPTER XV.

SUNDRY GOLD ALLOYS.

CHAPTER XVI.

CHOICE RECIPES.

CHAPTER XVII.

GOLD VALUES AND ALLOYS.

THE

JEWELLER'S ASSISTANT

IN THE

ART OF WORKING IN GOLD.

--- * ---

CHAPTER I.

**The Chemical and Physical Properties
of Gold.**

THERE can be no doubt that any information
emanating from the mind of a practical man, having a general bearing upon the various trades intimately connected with the art of gold and silver
working, will be exceedingly welcome to all who
have a desire to acquire knowledge not generally
met with in the mere mechanical working of the
several metals as *mechanical operations only*. For
careful observation and research are required to note
the facts, of which we are about entering into the
details.

To the successful practice of the art of gold and
silver working this information will be useful, in a
primary sense, to all practical mechanics who may
have occasion to work with or to treat the metals

B

in their pure state, although few metals have any application in the industrial arts in that condition.

We shall commence the subject with a description of the distinctive qualities of gold, the noblest of all the metals.

Fine Gold.

The characteristics of gold are remarkable in a high degree; when pure it has a very fine, rich orange-yellow colour, and is extremely ponderous. Fine gold has all the distinctive qualities of metals in their utmost perfection; it is infinitely *malleable*, for it can be extended in every direction by hammering and rolling; no metal extends so much as gold does, and under the manipulative skill of the goldbeater its noble qualities are at once apparent.

It is also exceedingly *ductile*, the most so of all the metals, and capable of being drawn into a thread or wire as fine as human hair without breaking by the exercise of proper care; when weighed in pure distilled water it loses between one-eighteenth and one-nineteenth part of its weight. It fuses at a temperature of 2016° Fahrenheit's thermometer, and although it may be kept for a long time in a state of fusion it loses nothing of its substance, even if the fire is kept at the greatest heat, as it is of a most fixed nature.

Pure, or fine gold, as it is called, gives no sound when it is struck, and when in the crucible it no sooner reaches a good white heat than it melts; when fused in the pot it looks of a sea-green colour at the surface.

Fluxes alter the colour of gold; borax renders it pale, and saltpetre has a tendency to deepen it; so also has salammoniac and common salt. The strongest nitric acid has no effect on fine gold, neither has any other single acid; *aqua-regia* is its proper solvent, consisting of a mixture of hydrochloric and nitric acids, in the proportion of two parts of the former to one part of the latter.

The colour of pure gold is unaffected by heat; it does not tarnish in air or water, either from the action of sulphuretted hydrogen or by oxidation, whereas when it is alloyed it turns black in annealing.

Gold is one of the metals known from the earliest times, and has always been the most valuable from the beginning of the world, and pro- bably the most widely diffused, as it is found in almost every country, and always exists in the metallic state, in most cases in beautiful crystals.

The specific gravity of gold varies from 19·25 to 19·50 when hammered, and according to the degree of compression it has received; gold alloys itself with nearly all the metals, but on account of its dearness its alloys are limited, and confined chiefly to purposes of jewellery where gold constitutes the greater portion of material. The old Egyptian symbol for gold is represented by the following mark ⊙, signifying divinity and perfection.

At the present day the true chemical name symbolical of gold is represented by the Latin word *aurum*. The real value of fine gold, if purchased in quantities of ten ounces and upwards, is £4 5s. 3d. per ounce.

To afford knowledge to those persons unacquainted with the various values of *refined gold*, we may state that it is charged for at a rate in proportion to the quantity it is desired to purchase, and in the best market, according to the scale of the following table :—

TABLE OF GOLD PRICES.

	£	s.	d.	
1 ounce and under 5 ounces .	4	5	0	per ounce.
5 ,, ,, 10 ,, .	4	5	6	,,
10 ,, ,, 50 ,, .	4	5	3	,,

Although, at the prices above quoted, the gold is supposed to be *pure*, it is never absolutely so, the expenses attending the operation of purification being so very great, and these being added in addition to the usual charges, would increase the cost of it too much above its legitimate trade value. Pure gold may be obtained by dissolving the standard gold of the currency in *aqua-regia*, which preparation has been described in a preceding article. It takes from three to four parts of the acid to dissolve one part of gold, and the operation is best performed by putting the mixture into a small German flask, with a rather long neck, and then adding the gold to be purified. The gold will now become dissolved if the acids are good; but if the action should be slow, remove the flask to a warm place—a sand-bath, for instance, will answer the purpose admirably.

When the dissolution of the gold has been thoroughly effected, pour the liquid into a shallow porcelain vessel, and again apply heat until it begins to thicken. A scum, or film, will at this stage of the process appear upon the surface. Immediately this part of the performance has been accomplished, remove the evaporating dish to a cooler place and allow the contents to go through nature's process of crystallisation. The crystals of gold are now to be dissolved in a quantity of clean cold water, the solution filtered, and to the latter a solution of proto-sulphate of iron (copperas) must be added as long as it produces a precipitate.

Under the action of this mixture the gold takes the form of a brown powder at the bottom of the vessel that holds the solution which is being operated upon. It takes about five units of iron to precipitate one unit of gold to this state of division, and it is a very delicate test of ascertaining the existence of gold in solution, producing a somewhat bluish tint in a mixture containing certainly not more than a 50,000th part of the precious metal. Standard gold, treated by the means just described, is produced in a form as near approaching absolute chemical purity as it is possible to get it.

Instead of evaporating the acid perchloride of gold solution to the state of crystallisation, it may be rendered neutral by the addition to it of a solution of caustic soda, and then precipitated with the mixture of iron above alluded to, but it is not so safe as the other, as minute atoms of gold may be still left in solution after the iron has chemically done its work. If preferred, the acid solution of perchloride of gold may be very largely diluted with water, and then effectually precipitated with the solution of iron in the same manner as before pointed out.

Gold alloys of 15 and 18 carats cannot so well be purified of their components when they contain various quantities of silver, as this latter metal sometimes resists the strongest *aqua-regia* in consequence of the dense chloride of silver which invariably forms itself on the surface of the article to be operated upon. In qualities of gold containing a very small proportion of this metal it is always, when treated by the *aqua-regia* process, precipitated in the first process of dissolving into a chloride of its metal by the action of the hydrochloric acid which forms the greater portion of the *aqua-regia* mixture, and falls to the bottom of the vessel containing the substance under *analysis*, from which it may be removed after the mixture has properly effected its object by decantation, or collected upon the filter, reference to which has been made in a former part of this subject.

In dissolving alloyed gold for the purpose of obtaining the metal in its pure state, the chemicals employed should be quite pure, and if the quality of the gold is known to be below the standard of fineness it should be treated at the outset of the operation in the following manner for the speedy separation of the several metals with which it may be alloyed :—If the alloy of gold to be parted should be of 15-carat quality, to one ounce of this compound add one ounce ten pennyweights of fine silver.

Place this mixture in a crucible and well incorporate it by fusion in a melting furnace, a little fine charcoal powder being added at the point of fusion, as a flux, in order to protect it from the action of the air, which would produce a scum upon the surface, making it a difficult matter to pour the metal cleanly and clearly from the crucible without loss or waste taking place. When this alloy is in a thoroughly melted state it should be well stirred with an iron stirrer, and then poured into a deep vessel of cold water, to which a rotary action has been communicated by stirring. The higher the crucible is held by the operator from the mouth of the vessel holding the water the better will be the *granulation* of the metal, and the finer will be the grains produced, which are more suitable for the next operation.

The operation of adding the requisite proportion of silver to an alloy of gold is called *inquartation*, and to reduce it to the best standard, for the process of parting, the alloy should contain, after fusion and granulation, about three parts of silver to one part of gold, or a little less, to act with the greatest exactitude, for the nitric acid employed in parting, or dissolving out, the baser metals is found to act best with about that amount of silver.

It is necessary that a certain relation should exist between the amount of the several metals of which the alloy to be operated upon is composed. In our

case we have taken a specific alloy of 15 carats, and
we have calculated the amount of silver to be added,
inclusively of the other baser metals with which
undoubtedly it would be alloyed; this, however, is
no obstacle in the way of obtaining perfectly accurate results, but rather an advantage, which will be
explained by-and-by.

One ounce of 15-carat gold should contain 12
dwts. 12 grs. of fine gold; therefore, three times
that amount will be 37 dwts. 12 grs., exactly
the amount we have advised when the 7 dwts.
12 grs. which the ounce of gold contained at
the commencement are added to the amount
named in the process of inquartation. If the
silver, or silver and copper, be not present in
sufficient quantity, the mixture will not be so completely attacked by the nitric acid; whilst if too
much of these metals exist in the alloy, the gold
remains after separation in a very fine powder, and
its collection for the purpose of ascertaining its
exact weight is a measure of extreme difficulty.

The process of parting to which we are now
alluding is more suitable for the direct manipulations of the jeweller's workshop, where the appliances for gold-parting are not, as far as our experience teaches us, at all numerous. The grains
of alloy produced in the previous operation are

collected together and put into a parting-flask. Into the flask then is added 9 ozs. of acid solution, composed of one part by measure of the purest nitric acid and two parts of water ; this is allowed to digest for half an hour or so, when the liquid mixture may be carefully drawn off and the residue washed with warm water.

When this has taken place, pour into the flask, which still contains the gold, more acid mixture, this time a little stronger than the last, in order to ascertain if all the baser elements have been entirely removed. This latter acid mixture may be composed of half acid and half water, and should be allowed to act upon the gold for a period of fifteen minutes, or more. Decant or draw off the liquid as before, and well wash the residue with warm water, which will remove all the base ingredients and acidness from the gold in the flask.

The various liquids drawn off, as well as the rinsings, should be carefully saved, as they contain the silver, &c., in solution, and which require separate treatment for their recovery; to this matter, however, we shall have occasion to subsequently return.

To get the pieces of gold—for if the inquartation process has been properly effected such will be the case—from the flask, warm it upon a sand-bath, and when the gold is thoroughly well dry pour it out on to a sheet of clean glazed paper; from this it can easily be collected and transferred to a crucible, and a good strong heat given to it in a muffle will soon unite the gold into sufficient adherence that it may be weighed up properly.   If all the work appertaining to the various processes connected with this art have been carefully accomplished, the gold will now be found in a perfect state of chemical purity.

Gold may be purified of the baser elements with which it may be alloyed by dissolving it in heated mercury, and then immersing the amalgam in a mixture of diluted nitric acid.   This solution, which should be prepared of one measure of nitric acid to three or four measures of water, will, when the temperature of it is increased by heat, gradually remove the mercury, silver, copper, lead, and other base metal from the gold, and leave the latter in a state of finely-divided metallic powder.

Before, however, the application of the gold-purifying mixture to the amalgam, the excess of mercury may be removed by pressing it through wash-leather; but this operation should be done with care, as it always carries a little gold along with it, to prevent the loss of which the excess of mercury should be collected and preserved, and may subsequently be used in the treatment of a fresh compound.

Sponge Gold.—Gold can be produced in the form of a light sponge, and quite pure, by the following method of preparation:—Take any given quality of gold, and well fuse it with its own weight of litharge (oxide of lead); granulate the mixture in the manner before recommended, collect the grains, and then dissolve the lead and the other alloy from the gold by boiling it for a long time in dilute nitric acid of the strength employed in treating the amalgams of gold and mercury; this leaves the gold, when the supernatant liquor—containing the several nitrates of the baser metals—has been removed, in the form of a light spongy mass at the bottom of the vessel in which the operation has been conducted. The mass of gold now only requires to be well washed with warm water to free it from all impurity and acidity.

Gold is acted upon in solution and precipitated into a metallic state by the following chemicals :—

Proto-sulphate of iron (green copperas of commerce) produces a brown metallic powder in an acid solution of gold largely diluted with water; or, if free acid be present, the same object may be effected by, firstly, rendering the solution of gold neutral by means of caustic soda or potash, and subsequently adding to it the prepared mixture of copperas, well stirring the whole at the time of this addition in order that the salt of iron may more effectually do its work, and that with the least amount of material; the right quantum which it takes is about five times the amount of iron salt to precipitate one amount of metallic gold.

Proto-chloride of tin in a neutral solution of gold, or one very largely diluted with water, produces a precipitate of gold in the form of a purple powder.

Nitrate of suboxide of mercury also produces a precipitate in a gold solution, taking the form of a black powder.

Oxalic acid in a perfectly neutral solution produces a precipitate of gold without the addition of the mixture containing the gold of another metal, as is the case with the above, in order to effect its reduction.

Metallic zinc, if suspended in waste gold solution, in clean bright sheets, other than cyanide solutions, will effect a precipitate of metallic gold, but the zinc requires to be suspended for some time, as the process is slow and the solution should not be disturbed during the period of suspension. The solutions treated in this way should be rendered slightly acid, if they are not so already, previously to the immersion of the zinc plates, in order to better, and more quickly, enable the latter to accomplish the required work.

CHAPTER II.

The Precipitation of Gold in Waste Solutions.

HAVING alluded to the principal *tests* for gold, and having also pointed out their various characteristics when applied to the liquid subtances which contain that metal, we are now led to make an observation or two with regard to the uses and action of *ammonia* in gold solutions, and we intend to treat upon this part of the subject more comprehensively.

We shall do so for two reasons; firstly, because many master jewellers deem it absolutely necessary to add to their gold solutions and waste waters, ammonia, previously to the solution of copperas, and the advantage claimed by them in favour of this addition is, that it neutralises the solution and thus easily prepares the way for the work of the copperas, when that test is applied for the precipitation of the gold; and, secondly, because remark has been made upon the absence of that salt, and the great advantages that are to be gained by its employment in the manufactories of jewellers, as a speciality for the recovery of gold, in that part of " The Practical Gold-worker" which treats principally upon the recovery of chemically-dissolved gold, or alloys of gold.

We have already remarked that *proto-sulphate of iron* precipitates gold in nearly all solutions, and certainly in all ordinary solutions of jewellers, with the exception of cyanide solutions, and that without any previous preparation of them to receive it.   If jewellers' waste gold solutions (which are contained in collecting-vessels appointed for the purpose) *really required* this point of neutralisation, the rinsing waters absolutely indispensable for so many gold-working purposes would be amply sufficient for every purpose whatsoever.

The surplus waters which accumulate in such large quantities in the collecting-vessels will render the acids employed in the gold-worker's art (no matter how strong, and however large in quantity) exceedingly dilute, even *if* the solutions were imperatively required in that weak state, for the purpose of promoting a precipitation with the chemical ingredient to which we have *specially* alluded in the work referred to.

Again, setting entirely on one side the observations above, for the sake of argument we will endeavour to show, further, the absurdity of the rigid adherence to the constant use of ammonia as a neutraliser for waste solutions, and its impracticability in some of the modes of subsequently treating the residue produced from its application.

Before directing attention, however, to this point, we may observe the fact, that carbonate of soda or potash is employed by art metal-workers in the manifold branches of their trades, and that these substances have not only the power of producing effective neutralisation in preserved waste solutions, but also the power of producing in hot solutions an actual precipitate of gold, &c.

It is thus shown that the large addition of water—in practice commonly known as rinsings—is a sufficient neutraliser to enable the copperas to most effectively perform the functions required of it, and in any single case, where the waste water should not happen to be in this state of dilution, the compulsory use of carbonate of soda in the washing-out of newly-polished, and some kinds of finished work, admirably completes the process the ammonia is supposed to effect, and that without producing any dangerous compound such as ammonia would produce, by precipitating gold as a fulminating powder, and which would be an exceedingly dangerous substance to deal with in collecting the residue into a metallic button; at least, if some of the methods now in operation for that purpose were employed.

In gold solutions this point of neutralisation *is only really* required when the mixture contains spirits of salts (muriatic acid) in some measure of strength, and *even* in cases of the latter description the carbonate of soda is all that is required in bringing about the desired result.

Writing on the precipitation of gold from waste water solutions, it brings to mind the following conversation held with a master jeweller, and for whom we once acted as foreman, upon our calling attention to the great advantages that were likely to accrue from the use of proto-sulphate of iron in the treatment of his waste waters; and here we wish to observe that all minute particles of dissolved gold were allowed to run away into the sewers, and knowing this, we naturally thought a great saving might be effected by our plan of precipitating the gold thus held in solution.

Upon unfolding our scheme he quietly remarked, " And what are you going to do with the pieces of iron? How are you going to get rid of them?" We

C

merely told him pieces of iron were not a part of our scheme, so far as they meant employment in that state, but that we proposed to employ a salt of iron in an aqueous condition, and make it an addition to the waste waters at regular intervals.

He remarked, " But then I don't see how you are going to get rid of the iron ?" We informed our employer that a portion of the salt contained nothing more than sulphuric acid, and this would be still held in solution in precisely the same manner as the other liquid substances, and that a very small portion of iron sufficed to effect the object we had in view—the precipitation of the gold—and this probably would go to the bottom of the collecting vessel with the gold, to be collected with the sediment which contained the gold. " But even then I don't see how you are going to part it from the gold ?" he went on. Our patience, after a time of useless discussion, being now nearly exhausted, we referred him, in answer to the last question, to the melters and refiners with whom he did business; and to the present day we believe a portion of his gold is allowed to run entirely away without any scientific method of recovery.

We continue our remarks on this subject, by extending them in the direction of the alloys of gold, or its various combinations with other metals,

all of which are very numerous. It is highly
interesting to know the multifarious compounds
which go to form the alloys of gold, especially
those combinations of metals which are prepared
wholly for the purpose of evolving special tints.

The alloys of gold with copper, with silver, and
with mercury, the latter forming *amalgam*, are the
most important of all the alloys of gold, but there
are other metallic elements which freely enter into
combination, forming homogeneous alloys with
gold, and may even be employed for commercial
purposes in such an art as the jeweller's. Among
some few of them we may mention such metals as
soft iron, zinc, platinum, composition (a mixture of
copper and zinc), &c., &c.

Copper and gold combine in all proportions,
but too large a proportion of the former element
materially affects the latter, by making it considerably redder in colour. It is by alloying in
this manner, that what is now known as red gold
is produced ; it is an alloy rather more difficult to
work with for some purposes, than when a certain
proportion of silver as well as copper enters into
the compound. Such an alloy as the former gives
increased hardness to gold and renders it much
more fusible, but not so much so as when silver
largely forms a part of the mixture ; in either case

the density is below that of fine gold, while the sonorousness is greatly increased.

Silver and gold may readily combine in any proportions, forming green, pale green, and white alloys, according to the various proportions of the former metal in the alloys produced.

Jewellers do not alloy their gold with too much silver, partly on the grounds of economy, and partly to please the tastes of their customers and the public generally, who like something rich looking for their money, and this rich-looking tint cannot be produced when too much silver is used in the alloy; and so it has happened, that jewellers are compelled to use a combination of metals in some of their golds, to satisfy this public taste.

In some instances jewels are made of various alloys of gold, each alloy showing a distinctive characteristic in the representation of colour, and when the articles are finished for the market, all these various hues or tints, produced in the first place by alloy, show themselves to the greatest perfection possible. Such instances as these are rare, it is true, and require the greatest judgment and care, on the part of every one connected with undertakings of that kind, in the production of the proper tints, and their suitability—so far as the several colours are concerned—to the design in course of execution.

We shall now direct attention to those useful metals which, when united with gold in stated proportions by fusion, serve to answer for the purposes of those alloys of which we have just been speaking ; and here we must observe that much greater care is required in the preparation of such compounds, than is the case with alloys pre-- pared and used by the major portion of the trade of manufacturing jewellers.

CHAPTER III.

The Different Colours of Gold.

YELLOW gold is pure or fine gold without any addition of alloy whatever.

PALE YELLOW GOLD.

	oz.	dwts.	grs.
Fine gold	o	18	8
Pure zinc	o	1	16
	1	0	0

This alloy is of 22-carat quality, and will cost about 78s. 2d. per ounce, calculating the cost of the gold in its pure state at 85s. 3d. per ounce. To this alloy, to keep up the proper standard, add 6 grs. extra per ounce of zinc for loss in the melting of it, as the zinc is very materially reduced in quantity during the fusion of the compound.

ANOTHER YELLOW GOLD.

	oz.	dwts.	grs.
Fine gold	o	18	8
Charcoal iron	o	1	16
	1	0	0

This alloy is of the same quality as the preceding one, costing about 78s. 2d. per ounce. It requires care in the preparation, and also in its subsequent treatment.

GREYISH YELLOW GOLD.

	oz.	dwts.	grs.
Fine gold	0	16	16
Charcoal iron	0	3	8
	1	0	0

This alloy is of 20-carat value, and costs 71s. 1d. per ounce. It requires the same care in the various stages of treatment as the one preceding it.

RED GOLD.

	oz.	dwts.	grs.
Fine gold	0	15	0
Swedish copper	0	5	0
	1	0	0

This alloy is of 18-carat quality, and costs 64s. per ounce. In the melting of this alloy very little is lost, it works without difficulty, and colours a deep colour, with a proper recipe, without loss.

GREEN GOLD.

	oz.	dwts.	grs.
Fine gold	0	15	0
Fine silver	0	5	0
	1	0	0

This alloy is also of 18-carat quality, but costs
65s. 3d. per ounce, on account of the high price of
silver which forms the ingredient of alloy. It is
easily melted and worked into any required form.
It is chiefly used for ornamentation in the shape of
leaves, and the characteristic green tint is given to
finished work by means of the graver.

BLUE GOLD.

	oz.	dwts.	grs.
Fine gold	o	15	o
Charcoal iron	o	5	o
	1	o	o

This alloy forms another of 18-carat quality,
costing about 64s. per ounce. It is very difficult to
melt, and may best be performed by dissolving
gradually iron wire in melted gold; a little extra
may be added to the given proportions, for loss,
say about 2 grs. of iron per ounce.

DEAD LEAF GREEN GOLD.

	oz.	dwts.	grs.
Fine gold	o	14	o
Fine silver	o	6	o
	1	o	o

This alloy is of a quality a little under 17 carats,
and costs 60s. 3d. per ounce. There is not much

difficulty about the preparation and subsequent
treatment of this alloy.

GREYISH WHITE GOLD.

	oz.	dwts.	grs.
Fine gold	o	12	12
Charcoal iron	o	7	12
	1	0	0

This alloy is of 15-carat quality, and costs 53s. 3d.
per ounce. It requires the treatment in all stages
as has been recommended in preceding alloys with
iron.

WATER GREEN GOLD.

	oz.	dwts.	grs.
Fine gold	o	12	0
Fine silver	o	8	0
	1	0	0

This alloy forms a quality nearly approaching
14½ carats, costing 53s. 3d. per ounce.

GREY GOLD.

	oz.	dwts.	grs.
Fine gold	o	10	0
Charcoal iron	o	10	0
	1	0	0

This alloy is of 12-carat quality, and will cost

about 42s. 8d. per ounce. The same treatment should characterize this alloy as we have already explained.

WHITE GOLD.

						oz.	dwts.	grs.
Fine gold .	.	.	.	.	.	0	10	0
Fine silver .	.	.	.	.	.	0	10	0
						1	0	0

Another 12-carat alloy, costing in this case 45s. 3d. per ounce. An alloy very simple in treatment in all the various processes of manipulation.

The colour of the various alloys of gold, more especially in demand at the present day for the manufacture of articles of jewellery, is that very nearly approaching to a red tint; such alloys are produced by the alteration of the baser ingredients which were formerly employed for the purposes of adulterating or lowering the purity of gold; and by a reduction of the more valuable metal, silver, with a proportionate increase of best red copper, to standard proportions, such purposes are readily effected.

Alloys so prepared are more difficult of fusion, and sometimes require very careful treatment in the working of them: and this feature is prominently experienced with those workmen who have

always been accustomed to work from pale gold
alloys. We are continually hearing complaints
of this kind outside our own business, and in
nine cases out of ten the fault is not that of the
gold or alloy, but owing to irregularities in the first
treatment.

Some copper alloys are unmistakably hard in
nature; to such alloys more frequent annealings
should certainly be given at the commencement
or period of breaking down of the bar of metal.
If this process be neglected at the time stated,
and although the gold may apparently be working all right, only a little hard "sir," the evil
effects of this wrong treatment will subsequently be
felt with tenfold force, when the finer processes of
dealing with it are put into operation. But then the
mischief is done, and past all remedy, save a return
to the melting-pot. Then the mischief is assigned
to the wrong cause, such as over-heating in the
melting; not enough borax employed; the alloy
not right, &c., &c.; and other like expressions;
whereas the real mischief was done by improper
manipulation.

This kind of thing we have seen proved before
us, and have ourselves guaranteed the success
of the undertaking before commencing upon it,
well knowing the capacity of the said alloy

from having worked up the material from which
that to be employed in the experiment was taken.
Sometimes gold alloys will be found a little cracky.
This is owing to two causes ; firstly, to too much
hardening pressure, which brings out and disunites
the fibres of the metal; and secondly, to a little
dirt or grit, which may accidentally have been
dropped into the crucible, either with the copper or
with the charcoal employed as flux.

To prevent in the future a repetition of these
drawbacks, use no other but the best and finest
vegetable charcoal procured from a respectable
establishment, and see that the copper is perfectly
clean and free from grit before it is made an
addition to the precious metals.

CHAPTER IV.

The Mixing and Melting of Gold.

HAVING reached this stage of our remarks, we now come to deal with a very important feature in the manufacture of some of the alloys of gold; we particularly refer to one of the most valuable of gold alloys—as regards intrinsic worth—18-carat, an alloy of three-fourths pure gold and one-fourth of inferior mixture. 18-carat gold, if alloyed with too little silver, is far more difficult to melt in a form that will turn out as malleable and as ductile as should essentially be the case with this quality of gold; now this difficulty is not nearly so apparent when a little more silver is employed in the composition; neither is it so when one of the alloying ingredients is absent from the mixture altogether; all this has been, however, exhaustively dealt with in our work for goldsmiths entitled "The Practical Goldworker."

A few more details, while we are upon this subject, will not be considered misplaced, because

many of our correspondents do not appear to have
mastered this question of 18-carat gold preparing ;
and, secondly, because a correspondent has just applied to us for information upon this very question.

The question is : " Why does 18-carat gold
always crack if prepared with Australian sovereigns, yet the same when reduced to 9-carat
quality works all right ?" Now the question is a
simple one, and yet very difficult to answer on
paper in the absence of further information than
that contained in the above note of interrogation.

In the first place, it is always more difficult to
melt small quantities of 18-carat gold than large
ones, so as to work in a proper manner; then,
again, too little silver may have been employed
in the mixture, in which case the grain of the
metal will appear, when broken, of a sandy red
colour, and very coarse in texture; this shows that
the various ingredients used for the preparation
have not properly and chemically united to each
other, for being very readily disunited by pressure,
proves such to have been the case; whereas, if
proper chemical unition had taken place in the
fusion of the compound, the subsequent pressure
brought to bear upon the metal would have com-
pressed the fibres together into smaller space, thus
rendering the material still more tenacious and

workable. The reason why 9-carat quality is more easily prepared and worked is a much simpler problem to 'fathom ; the large proportion of alloy which must necessarily be added to make the quality named brings the mixture, ordinarily speaking, to a more perfect state of homogeneity, as consisting of similar atoms, or elements of a like nature, which are not so easily separated as are those in the above-named alloy, when a proper chemical composition has not been considered in relation thereto.

To proceed to the details of 18-carat alloys made from Australian sovereigns, we may observe that silver is used almost exclusively for alloying in the manufacture of those coins by the officials of the colonial mints of Sydney and Melbourne, in Australia ; this, of course, may, if preferred, necessitate a little less of that material being employed in the process of their reduction to 18-carat quality, but too great advantage should not be taken of this fact, if the evil of which our correspondent complains is to be avoided.

There is no reason whatever to prevent Australian coins from being thus employed, if practical knowledge is brought to bear upon the subject. We have ourselves used them for all qualities of gold, and that without a single drawback attending them. In alloying gold, or in other words, in reducing Australian sovereigns to 18-carats, for a simple alloy, take a given number of coins, which will prevent the cutting of them, as follows :—

Good 18-carat alloy—

	oz.	dwts.	grs.
Four Australian sovereigns . . .	1	0	12
Fine silver	0	2	6
Swedish copper	0	2	6
	1	5	0

This alloy will stand hall-marking, and it contains about 3 dwts. of silver per oz., when calculated in conjunction with that which the coins contain, and it will produce an alloy, if proper manipulative skill is employed, of very fair workable capacity, and of an exceedingly rich-looking pale yellow colour.

Continuing our remarks upon the subject of 18-carat gold alloys, their various preparations for the crucible, and the general mechanical and manipulative details belonging to them, permit us here to state that it requires a certain amount of practical knowledge to produce in good condition from the melting, alloys of gold of the proportions of material of which 18-carat is known to consist, without the defective appearance showing itself upon the surface, of which our correspondent speaks, and which so visibly presents itself upon subsequent pressure being applied to the bar of metal, *even* with such alloys as we have advised, unless very careful treatment be observed in the process of fusion, and in the pouring of the mixture from the crucible.

We have known instances in which several jewellers of our acquaintance always adopted the precautionary measure of twice melting their 18-carat alloys before attempting the mechanical process of working them. The process was performed in this way : the proportions of gold, silver, and copper were taken and put into the melting-pot for fusion ; when this had taken place, and the mixture was in a perfectly liquid state, the crucible was withdrawn from the furnace, and the contents carefully poured into an open ingot, which had previously been heated up to a certain temperature for its reception. The crucible was immediately put back again into the furnace, and the bar of gold upon being removed from the open ingot with a pair of iron tongs, was at once transferred to it for a second fusion ; the pouring this time taking place in an ingot arranged in the manner peculiar to the reception of gold and silver.

We are not prepared to say whether there is any advantage to be gained by such a procedure, but

D

this much is certain, that bars of 18-carat gold,
prepared by the means stated, have exhibited all
the defects of which numbers of jewellers have
repeatedly and bitterly complained ; and whom we
are endeavouring to assist, by supplying information of a really practical character, which may be
of service to them in a pecuniary sense. In further-
ance of this object we will give to our readers who
desire such information an alloy of 18-carat gold
quality, which has invariably been found free from
all workable defects.

An alloy, with Australian sovereigns, has already
been given in these pages, but it may not always
be convenient to procure these for the purpose of
alloying ; to supply this inconvenience the following alloy is given with *fine gold* as the principal ingredient, in the place of the Australian sovereign as
heretofore given.

Good 18-carat alloy, with fine gold.

	oz.	dwts.	grs.
Fine gold	1	0	0
Fine silver	0	4	0
Swedish copper	0	2	16
	1	6	16

This alloy will contain about the same proportion
of silver per oz. as the one with Australian sove-

reigns, *i.e.* 3 dwts. to the oz. of material when alloyed and prepared to the manufactured state. It may be used for bright gold purposes of finishing or for colouring, for either of which purposes it is admirably suited and works exceedingly well, being smooth, firm, and tenacious, and of a pale yellow colour when polished.

CHAPTER V.

The Dry-Colouring of Gold.

SINCE our last articles appeared upon the subject of 18-carat gold mixtures for various purposes, several of our correspondents have experienced a difficulty in producing excellent results, so far as manipulating with them for a purpose other than those laid down in our previous remarks. It appears that *dry-colouring* is coming much into fashion, no doubt on account of the highly-finished surface of articles prepared for the market by such a process.

The very bright and rich-looking appearance attained by this means as compared with the *dead* surface of *wet-colouring*, is one of the reasons why articles so finished are being asked for by shopkeepers and others, with the idea of tempting the purchasing public with something to all appearance new and different looking to those generally offered to them for sale. Now, to produce this richness and evenness of surface to the greatest possible perfection, a special mixture should be employed for the work upon which it is to be produced, not only as regards the ingredients, which have to form the colouring paste, but also those of the alloy of which the work is composed ; therefore, it must not naturally be supposed that a good alloy which produces all the desired results in *wet-colouring* will do so by manipulation under the regulations which govern this new process, and which is entirely different in its action and preparation to that commonly and formerly employed in the trade of a goldsmith. Yet this is what has been expected of an alloy more fit for bright gold purposes of finishing than *even* for wet-colouring, by workmen whose everyday experience should have taught them more wisdom.

In wet-colouring, to bring to the surface a presentable and uniform appearance involving a speciality of tint, an alloy is required capable of not only materially assisting the colouring mixture in effecting this, but it is also of the utmost importance that the chemicals employed for this purpose should be so selected and arranged in manipulation that the action of the one be perfectly suited to the other ; and this must be so in every case if all the best results are to be achieved by the process of which we are speaking.

Now, in dry-colouring, it is even more imperatively necessary that these principles or regulations should have careful and proper attention paid to them by the operator who is about to perform the process, unless he desires to see his work come from the colour-pot *patchy*, or with a white film upon the surface, which is much to be guarded against.

Our idea of what a workman should be is this: he should not only be competent to perform the various duties of his trade *mechanically*, but also be enabled to explain the *rationale* of every process appertaining to his art. In order to afford some little assistance to our fellow-workers by forwarding their advancement in the craft to which we have the honour to belong, we will endeavour to explain more closely the general details of the subject bearing upon the preceding observations.

Wet-colouring is a process that considerably reduces in weight any articles submitted to its action, and this reduction, which takes place from the surface, is far more apparent in proportion to the poorness of the alloy, the amount of silver contained therein, and the strength of and length of time the colouring mixture is employed. By the strength we mean the quantity of acid used in proportion to a given quantity of alkaline salts. The greater the proportion of silver per oz. in the alloy to be operated upon in wet-colouring, the greater should be the quantity of acid, and *vice versâ.* Why is this necessary? may be asked. We reply, because it is imperative that some strong mixture should be employed in order to break up the fragments of silver which underlie the surface more or less of all coloured gold work.

Now, while silver is more resisting to the action of muriatic acid than copper, it very readily, when used in conjunction with a little common salt or sal-ammoniac, effects the desired purpose of breaking up and removing from the surface of the work all traces of that and other extraneous matter, leaving behind what, to all appearance, constitutes a pure gold-like surface, though dull and uniform. Whereas in the process of dry-colouring very little, if any, is removed from off the articles, the mixture employed not having the power chemically to do so ; it proves that if a fine deep orange colour be desired upon the work very little silver should enter into the alloy employed, for it only removes that depth of shade from the articles which is so essential should be maintained in every stage of manufacture, and which every one fails to produce in the finish when guided by wrong considerations.

The pale colour sometimes seen on articles of first-class jewellery which have been finished by the process of colouring, commonly styled *dry-*

colouring, is not the result of any inferiority of the quality of the material of which they are composed, but due to the chemically resisting properties imparted to it by the incorporation of the various proportionate parts of metals generally employed in rendering complete the formation of the mixture, in order that it may possess in a remarkable degree all those qualities of flexibility and ready compliance, qualities which are all in all to the jeweller, in a more or less marked manner, in every branch of his art. From a mechanical standpoint all these qualities are specially desired by the art-worker in gold and the precious metals.

Now the preparation of an alloy not only adds to and detracts from these qualities in accordance with the order of its composition, but it has, likewise, a very great deal to do with the numerous shades of colour that are collectively produced by the trade; and any special mode of mixing by a firm consequently brings its own *specialité* of colour; thus, under the operations of a skilful and practised hand, we may have very nearly every shade of colour artistically worked out by a careful manipulation in gold, and *gold and its alloys*.

The pale colour of gold work, which is not so rich-looking and pleasing to the taste in comparison with a deeper tint, is often produced in ignorance of the scientific principles which naturally point to the cause of its production. We have frequently been informed of the utter inability of even practical persons to prevent this paleness upon their work, and we have now before us abundance of proofs in support of this very testimony, in the shape of correspondence bearing upon the particular point at issue, the writers of which we have been enabled to assist by supplying them with particulars regarding the cause of failure.

In one case submitted we have an alloy of full 18-carat value, containing as much as 15 per cent. of silver per ounce. Now, considering that the mixture for dry-colouring has only a very weak affinity, or chemical attraction, for the metals in its special mode of employment, such mode forming the process, it will be at once apparent, even to the most unobservant, that so large a percentage of silver must carry its tint, to a considerable extent, to and from the colour-pot in which the experiment has taken place. When it is known that the silver in this alloy predominated something like 5 per cent. over the copper, there can be no surprise expressed at the work finishing pale by those well-informed upon the subject.

The principal cause of pale gold, as produced by the dry-colouring process, having now been explained, it will be necessary to call attention to some of the subsequent devices employed in attempted improvements of this paleness, so as to bring to the surface a deeper and richer colour to the work.

Of late years wet-coloured work, and burnished so as to produce a smooth, mirror-looking surface, has been pushed into the market as goods bearing the dry-coloured surface upon them. Not at all has the device been invented with the view of deceiving the public in the quality of their goods, but because operatives have been unable to produce by the older method that tone or depth of colour required to satisfy the public taste—a taste now vastly improved as regards former requirements, in the direction of a more artistic manner of finishing, as well as a much richer and deeper shade of colouring.

It should now be a well-known fact that genuine dry-colouring cannot be effected with all the elements of success upon work inferior to 18-carat gold quality; whereas, with wet-colouring and subsequently burnishing, a similar colour may be made to appear upon all qualities amenable to the wet-colouring mixtures of the period. The only effective check upon this kind of finishing jewellery work with which we are at the present acquainted is its liability to detract, in a permanent sense, from the richness primarily imparted to it, by its diminished lustre.

Iron ladles were formerly used as utensils for holding the colouring mixture, and being very convenient to manipulate with, the handle serving to facilitate the process of access to and removal from the fire in which the operation was conducted, they became at the time very general in all dry-colouring processes.

The iron of which they were composed, it was assumed, greatly assisted the mixture in the giving of a deeper and richer shade of colour to the work. This theory, no doubt, was true to some extent, and answered the purpose satisfactorily, anterior to the date in which modern art had been made to display the power wonderfully combined in the action of certain metals, particularly suited to the objects sought for.

Ladles appeared to answer nearly all the requirements the goldsmiths desired readily enough, the only practical drawback, and this was a real one, being found to exist when manipulating with a large batch of work; the ladle being considerably shallower towards the sides, it presented the difficulty of a portion of the work farthest from the centre exposing itself above the colouring mixture;

therefore, it either necessitated smaller batches of
work and the process more frequently applied, or
the devising of some more suitable vessel to hold
the mixture, the shape of which would conform to
a degree to the batch of work when large in
quantity. The latter method was adopted. This
improvement took practical form in the present
shaped colour-pot, although it was first made in
iron, operators then preferring iron as the best
material to employ.

In colouring with the iron ladle or iron pot, a
very much duller and deader colour was produced
upon the work than that of the present period. It
was usual to well rinse the work after colouring,
and then the only other subsequent process was
that of drying, which finally completed the work.
There was no scratching or burnishing in use at
that period of the goldsmith's art.

The colour much resembles that to be seen upon
Etruscan jewellery, and was effected by the use of
various mixtures. Of course it must be understood
that it was all 18-carat gold that was so treated,
all of which varied with different masters, as now,
both in the proportion of ingredients and methods
of application.

The following was a very good mixture in use at
the time of which we speak, and produced the

Etruscan colour so much desired by workers in that art with very little difficulty. The ingredients generally employed consisted of:—

Nitrate of potassa (saltpetre) . . .	6 parts.
Common salt (table)	6 ,,
Sulphate of iron (copperas) . . .	1 ,,
Sulphate of zinc (white vitriol) . . .	1 ,,
Sulphate of alumina (alum) . . .	1 ,,
Total . . .	15 parts.

All these were pulverised to a fine powder, and intimately well mixed together with the hands, and then transferred to the iron ladle for fusion, or otherwise, for the dissolution of them in their water of crystallisation. The work, having been well prepared to take the colour, was dipped into the rising mixture and turned about two or three times, and then withdrawn and rinsed in hot water, or water containing a small portion of one of the corrosive acids, which dissolved any colour that adhered to the work. The drying of the work in hot boxwood sawdust finished all manufacturing processes, and the work should then, if perfect, be free from all spots or blemishes and of a uniform rich dull colour.

Another very good mixture for producing the Etruscan gold colour consisted as follows :—

Saltpetre	5 ounces.
Alum	2 ,,
Sulphate of zinc	1 ,,
Sulphate of iron	1 ,,
Total . . .	9 ounces.

These ingredients may be treated according to either of the following methods with varying success. Dissolve the salts in their water of crystallisation, using an iron ladle or other suitable vessel to contain the liquid, which, when dissolved and about to rise up a little, the work should be laid in for a short time, then gently turned about, and subsequently withdrawn. If the colour is not then dark enough the experiment should be repeated, and as often until the desired colour is brought to the surface, though usually two or three dips is considered sufficient for the purpose.

The other method of treatment to which we have alluded was performed in a still more simple manner, viz., the ingredients were at the outset ground to a fine powder and mixed with a small quantity of water so as to form only a very thick paste; this paste was then either brushed over the articles to be coloured, or the latter were dipped into it, in order that they may become well coated with the mixture, without which the work would probably finish patchy. This part of the process having been performed, the articles were next placed upon a clean pan of copper or iron, and at once submitted to the action of a clear coke fire; this action was allowed to go on until the colour began to burn.

The process may be ascertained to have proceeded far enough when black smoke is being transmitted from the work upon the pan. At this period the pan is withdrawn from the fire, its contents allowed to cool, and then immersed in water, to which a small quantity of sulphuric acid had previously been added; this latter removed any flux or other impurity adhering to the surface. A final rinsing in clean water, to which a very little carbonate of potash had been added, and drying well the work, absolutely finished the whole process. And if the alloy had been all right a fine, deep, uniform colour would be the result of the operator's labour.

To produce a soft, deep colour on jewellery work the alloy should contain a very large preponderance of copper, and should be weakly coloured, whether the process be performed by the *dry* or *wet* process, to insure certain success.

Twenty-carat gold is a very good and medium alloy for all dry-colouring purposes, and it is a fully recognised standard quality in Ireland, capable of bearing the Government *hall-marks* attached to that quality of gold. In the treating of this standard it is easier to produce a good colour than when treating with the lower standard of 18-carats, however variously the former may be alloyed with the respective metals commonly employed by gold-smiths for alloying purposes; still, even with this alloy, when too great a proportion of silver is employed, the chances against producing an eminently satisfactory colour are considerably increased.

A far greater proportion per ounce, however, may confidently be employed in proportion to the copper, because the alloy would be much richer in the amount of gold than the one of 18 carats; and this has a marked tendency to effect, more easily and effectually, those high results with regard to finish which all aim at.

One of the earliest and most common recipes for enriching the surface of high-quality gold, when this mode of finishing jewellers' work became fashionable, used, either in its employment for the purpose of ornamentatien in contrast to the former method of bright-finishing, or as a desirable mode of altering the naturally pale colour of polished gold work, of inferior quality, by imparting to it the colour of very fine gold. To accomplish the latter purpose the following chemical salts were employed in various ways, and were found to produce satisfactory and serviceable results. with the legally workable quality allowable at that period of the goldsmith's art in this country; a standard of which had previously been enacted by the Legislature for the guidance of jewellers, and any one found manipulating with an inferior quality committed an offence highly improper.

The colouring salts compounding the mixture should all be prepared *chemically* pure, and may be taken in the following proportions, which make a good colour if applied in a proper manner, and that to a suitable alloy of the standard quality, viz., 22-carat :—

Saltpetre	6 ounces.
Alum	3 ,,
Salt	3 ,,
Sulphate of zinc	3 ,,
	15 ounces.

The ingredients are first of all reduced to a fine powder, and well mixed together in order to procure a thorough union; a little water is then added, and the whole stirred well together; the water should be added little by little, well stirring after each addition, care being taken not to make the colouring paste too liquid, which is very objectionable to the process. The paste should be, when properly prepared, of the thickness and consistency of

E

cream. In this state it attaches itself more firmly
to the work, the surface of which only it acts upon
and deepens; but always remember, in proportion
to the nature and goodness of the gold alloy, *i.e.*
the smaller the amount of base alloy which the
article contains, and, still more, the smaller the
amount of silver in that base alloy, so will be, in
proportion, the depth and richness of colour imparted to the work at the close of the process
performed.

The work, which is prepared chemically clean by
the action of acids upon it, is now taken and
dipped into the paste, or otherwise well rubbed
over with it, so as to leave no part exposed from
the mixture, and subsequently placed upon a clean
copper pan (copper being decidedly the best) and
heated until all hissing or crackling noise has sub-
sided; in fact, the heat should be continued until
the colouring paste has actually become fused to
the surface of the work, when it may be withdrawn
and plunged into acidulated pickle water, which
dissolves the salts and throws up the high and rich
tint of pure gold. If the colour is not deep enough
the process should be repeated, though it is seldom
required but once if the alloy is right and the gold
good in quality.

Such a process as the above is only fit to be

employed upon very rich gold, such, for example, as 22-carat gold, if good commercial results are to be accomplished. The film of colouring paste is very thin, and consequently can bestow very little action on the surface of the work. This and similar gold-colouring processes are very often given in scientific periodicals and published books, without a sufficient amount of real practical detail of the facts here laid down as to the *specialité* of the alloy and the quality of the gold, and without such information as we are supplying; such recipes are consequently utterly worthless to amateurs and scientific experimentalists, because, through having been applied by them to some unsuitable alloy and quality, their labours have resulted in complete failure.

With 22-carat gold the process here described can be accomplished with a very fair amount of success, but with any lower quality the results would, we are quite sure, be very indifferent to that produced by other processes for accomplishing the same object, viz., the enriching and beautifying of the surface of alloyed gold.

To modern processes we shall refer hereafter, together with some of our own experiments, which have been sought for with the view of economical improvements in the art of gold-colouring; our

aim being at present to point out the defects of
gold-work manipulations as acquired from book
learning, and to show the advantages which may
be derived from their *proper* application, by supplying the necessary information which usually
unaccompanies these *recipes*, as they appear to be
copied in the words of unpractical authors, one
after the other, most of whom never, probably,
manipulated a piece of gold-work in their whole
lives, and whose information, therefore, is most
unreliable, in a commercial sense, for the successful
practice of an art which requires, more than any
other, exact, careful, and trustworthy information
upon so important a branch as this one of gold-
colouring.

The above ingredients and proportions, if prepared and mixed together, and then put into a
black-lead colour-pot and heated until dissolved in
their water of crystallisation, will effectually colour
20-carat gold, and even 18-carat gold may be
coloured in this mixture; but the solder must be
very good in quality to effect an even colour to the
surface.

When the salts are dissolved, which should be
done gradually, the mixture will rise up in the pot,
and then is the time for the immersion of the work,
which must be gently moved about for a minute or

so, and then withdrawn and immediately dipped into a pickle of nitric acid and water at nearly the boiling point.

If the colour on the surface of the work is not intense enough, the water should be well shaken from it and another dip must take place to bring up the proper colour, and with 18-carat gold alloys sometimes a third dip is even rendered necessary to raise the colour to the desired point of perfection. The rinsing-water, or pickle, may be of the strength of one of acid to twenty of water, and may be made by boiling the water and adding the acid to it.

Twenty-two-carat gold articles, such as a wedding-ring, or keeper, or anything small and plain, may be coloured by a very simple plan, as follows : Place the article upon a pumice-coke or piece of wood charcoal, and make it red-hot by blowing upon it the blow-pipe flame from a gas-jet, and afterwards boiling it out in a mixture of sulphuric acid and water, tolerably strong, say, in the proportion of one of acid to four of water, in a copper or other suitable vessel. If the colour is desired to be dead, the heating and boiling out should be repeated until a thoroughly uniform surface presents itself upon its removal from the boiling-out mixture.

When an even surface has been thus procured,

simply washing it in a hot solution of soap and water, with a clean and soft brush, completes the process. If desired bright, it may be scratched or burnished, then rinsed in the usual manner and dried in hot box-wood sawdust. A little— very small quantity—of potash added to the wash- ing-out waters improves the tone of colour, as well as completely neutralises the acid that may accidentally remain upon the articles through im- perfect rinsing in the swilling waters.

This method can only be successfully employed when a tolerably deep rich colour is a special requi- site to the finish of the work in hand, and then, *that can only* be effected with 22-carat gold alloys. Therefore, inferior alloys of gold to the one above named must not be treated with this recipe if an intense colour is aimed at by the operator in charge of the process.

Instructions in the art of colouring gold have frequently been given by various writers in high class journals of popular renown. Among some dozens we have noticed, we select the following extracts from well-known authors, with their names appended. Professor Church, Royal Agricultural College, Cirencester, says, in " Cassell's Popular Educator," " Gold, if not alloyed very much (not more than 9 parts in 24), may be made to assume

its proper colour by a process of 'pickling' or
'colouring.' Gold articles plunged when warm
into nitric acid lose a portion of their superficial
alloy, be it copper or silver, the pure metal being
left with a somewhat *matt* or dead surface and a
rich orange colour." Again he says, speaking of
the same quality of gold, " A mixture of equal
parts of borax, nitre, and sal-ammoniac, may be
made, ground into fine powder, mixed with a little
water, and applied as a thin coating to the metal.
The metallic object is then heated till a faint dis-
colouration appears on the coating ; afterwards, the
paste being washed off, the pure gold film will
appear beneath."

Mr. William Chaffers, in his work entitled " Hall
Marks on Gold and Silver Plate," has given, for
the benefit of jewellers and others, the following
paragraph which we copy *in extenso*:

" Coloured gold (of which cheap jewellery is made)
means that the article contains a very small proportion of gold, less frequently than 9-carat gold,
or 9 parts pure and 15 alloy out of the 24, which is
intrinsically worth about 30s. per ounce. As this
debased gold is of a bad colour and wanting in
brilliancy, the following operation is adopted, called
colouring: From the immediate surface of the article
the copper is removed, exposing the pure gold

only, but this coating of pure gold is not thicker
than the 100th part of the breadth of a hair. It is
the same as if the article were gilt or electro-plated,
only that in the one instance the alloy is *taken from*
the gold on the surface, leaving the pure gold,
and that in the *other* the pure gold is *put on*. Any
bad gold over 9 carats can be coloured by boiling
in nitric acid, or other preparation acting in the
same manner." Mr. Alfred Lutschannig, in his
" Book of Hall Marks," also makes use of these
latter observations of Mr. Chaffers with respect to
gold-colouring.

Now, more erroneous remarks than these never
existed for one moment in the mind of the practical and experienced gold-worker ; and it is really
astonishing that these and similar statements—
which we could quote—should go so long unchal-
lenged ; appearing as they do in works so well
known as those to which we have called attention.

We simply say, without any comment whatever, that nitric acid will produce no such effect
upon 9-carat gold as indicated. Indeed, the colour
of 9-carat gold, placed under such treatment, would
be more the colour of alloyed silver than that of
fine gold on the surface. Further, no alloyed gold
can be treated in such a manner for the production
of a good commercial colour, save and except

22-carats, reference to which has already been
made in former pages.

The colour effected upon 18-carat gold, however
deep it may be alloyed, when submitted to the above
modus operandi, is always very pale. Nevertheless,
a certain richness is imparted to it, which sometimes makes it very effective looking; but it does
not, in any case, produce a sufficiently deep, rich-
looking colour for general commercial purposes,
and therefore it cannot be safely recommended to
the practical gold-worker.

A mixture such as the following may be applied
with advantage, and if a moderate amount of skill
be employed during the operation, certain success
is sure to follow the process when red 18-carat
gold jewellery is treated with it. The ingredients
employed are as follows, when small work is to be
heightened in colour :—

Saltpetre	6 ounces.
Common salt	3 ,,
Alum	3 ,,
	12 ounces.

A colour-pot or crucible is provided with straight
sides, into which is put the salts, which should
have been previously well pulverised and mixed

together with the hands. Now place the colour-pot upon the fire (a gas jet is by far the best substitute, as the power of heat can be regulated at will, without the removal of the colour-pot from the position in which it was first placed), and dissolve the mixture very carefully and slowly so as not to burn the colouring composition. Stir occasionally during the dissolution of the salts.

When the latter have dissolved, the mixture will rise up somewhat in the pot, and then is the time to place in the work, which must be suspended by a wire of platinum of suitable dimensions to the work in hand. The work should be gently moved about while in the pot, and now and again withdrawn to inspect the colour of it.

Dipping in acid water removes any colour that adheres to the surface of the work, and which occasionally prevents a proper and satisfactory inspection of it. The acids used mostly for the purpose are nitric, muriatic, and sulphuric; either one may be used in the proportion of one of acid to twenty of boiling water. Be careful in adding the sulphuric to the water, as it will fly about in coming in contact with hot water, and scald or burn if it happens to alight on the flesh or clothes of the operator.

The water hanging to the work, after each rinse,

should be well shaken from it before re-dipping in the colour-pot. The time occupied in the process, if the alloy and other particulars absolutely necessary to the true performance are in accord, will be about four to five minutes.

After the dissolution of the colouring salts, the heat kept up should not be too intense during the period occupied in colouring; if so, the paste or composition is not at all unlikely to become devoid of the necessary moisture before the allotted time has expired, which, practically, is required to the termination of the treatment. A very slow fire, or, still better, a gas jet, is best for the purpose of accomplishing the common object in view, viz., the highest and richest colour to the work under treatment, and that in the simplest and easiest manner possible.

This colouring mixture may be employed for 16-carat, and also for as low as 15-carat gold, if the alloys are red gold ones. But for such a purpose its preparation and application are somewhat different to that just described, as well as to the length of time occupied in the process.

For a small batch of work the quantities may be the same as those already stated, although larger quantities can be used with the same success that attends the smaller ones, taking extra work in

proportion to increase of colour. The best relation
between the work and the colour would be as one
to three, four and five; that is, the mixture given
will be sufficient to colour four ounces of solid
work, such as chains, three ounces of hollow work,
or two ounces of light work, with large surfaces.
Always remember that it is in proportion to the
surface of the work that you have to provide a
colouring mixture, and not to its absolute weight,
to be accurate and correct in your results.

In colouring with the two inferior qualities
named above it is necessary to add water to the
salts in the pot, in order to keep them moist during
their period of action, which takes a much longer
time than the one we have already given the details
of to produce a colour intense enough for the
trades. Two ounces of water will be sufficient to
put to the mixed salts, which must be allowed to
boil. When this takes place, take the batch of
work, encircled with a wire of platinum or of silver,
and put it in the mixture, and there let it remain
for about fifteen minutes, when it should be withdrawn and instantly plunged into boiling water
provided in a pan for the purpose.

The work during the above period may occasionally be withdrawn and rinsed in order to inspect its
progress; and sometimes this is found to be an

advantage, as the right colour is produced more quickly at times than others. At the expiration of the above time it is a desirable plan to well scratch-brush the work in the usual manner, after which process it must especially be well rinsed when it is desired to re-dip it; and this is often the plan adopted by a good practitioner, when the colour is not deep enough, to give another dip for five minutes, when a beautiful colour is invariably the result. Scratching the articles, rinsing in plenty of clean water, and finally drying in box-wood sawdust, complete the operation.

CHAPTER VI.

The Wet-Colouring of Gold.

IN colouring 15, 14, 13, or 12½ carat gold, the same mixture may be employed, and for these qualities it is necessary to add a small quantity of muriatic acid to the water recommended in the last colour in order to produce the golden tint higher, and enough that is for commercial purposes. The acid should be of the strength of 1 in 8; and in order to secure a *lasting gold colour* to the work, it should be exposed to the action of the colour for a period ranging from seven to ten minutes, according to the quality of the gold and the nature of the alloy of which the work is composed. The alloys in the tables herein given are admirably suited to any of these processes, being extra red gold ones, and with which better results are effected.

The finishing of the work after any of these methods of colouring may be according to the purpose for which the work is intended. As there are various ways of finishing coloured work it will be as well to name them. The one in most general use is scratching at the lathe with a circular brass wire brush, upon which runs a mixture of ale and water, producing a slippery substance, which glides over the surface of the work, rendering it bright and smooth, or dead frosted, in accordance as the revolutions of the brush come in contact with it.

Another method is to burnish the work, using suitable tools of steel and agate to accomplish it with. The same mixture as for scratching may be employed to enable the tools to glide easily over the surface, or one of soft soap may be used if preferred; washing the work out with a solution of soap and hot water to which a little potash is added; using a clean soft brush, is another method, and each one imparts a rich and altogether different-looking surface to the work. For the latter process especially, the colouring is required to be perfectly uniform in appearance and without blemish.

We have lately introduced several new processes for surface finishing coloured and gilt work, and as we believe these methods are at present unknown outside our own workshop, we shall for the present refrain from describing them; our sole reason for keeping them secret being a desire to maintain and not lower present prices, which we are afraid would

soon be the case if we indiscriminately gave the
trade and the public the full benefit of our latest
knowledge, and that instead of encouraging technical skill in the manufacture of gold wares, it
might result in much keener competition and a corresponding loss of profit, a thing not at all to be
desired.

The following formula may be used with every
advantage in colouring the higher qualities of gold
alloys :—

Saltpetre	12 ounces.
Common salt	6 ,,
Alum	6 ,,
Water	$3\frac{1}{2}$,,
Muriatic acid . · . . .	$0\frac{1}{2}$,,
	28 ounces.

The salts used in this process are reduced to a fine
powder and transferred to the colour-pot along with
the water, and then heated until the boiling point
has been reached, when the muriatic acid is added,
the mixture again boiled and the work dipped into
the boiling colour, where it should remain from
seven to ten minutes. During this period the work
may occasionally be removed from the colour-pot
and rinsed in clean hot water in order to ascertain
how it is progressing. This produces a splendid

old-fashioned colour to the work so seldom seen now. Different tints are produced by shortening or lengthening the time of dipping.

Another formula for the lower qualities of gold, and with even as low as 12½-carat gold it answers admirably with the alloys recommended in this work for colouring purposes :—

Saltpetre	16 ounces.
Common salt	8 ,,
Muriatic acid	2 ,,
Water	6 ,,
	32 ounces.

The acid strength of this mixture is 1 in 4, or twice the strength of the former mixture. The ingredients of which it is composed should be reduced to a fine powder in a mortar, keeping them perfectly clean all the time; then take a blacklead colour-pot about seven inches high, and which has been well annealed; put the salts into it and add sufficient hot water to reduce them into a thick creamy paste; when this is done place the pot upon the fire, or upon a gas jet, and slowly boil up the mixture. At this stage add the muriatic acid, and when it boils up again, place the work which is to be coloured, and which has previously been prepared quite clean and free from grease, in the colour for

F

four minutes, keeping it gently on the move all the time, but not allowing it to touch the sides of the pot, which would scratch and spoil the work.

At the end of this time it must be withdrawn and instantly plunged into a vessel of boiling water, and afterwards into a second vessel of the same. Next place the work in the colour for two minutes longer, and again rinse well, as before directed, in fresh clean boiling water, and dry in clean box-wood sawdust. One or other of the finishing processes are next applied, but as directions have just been given there is no need to repeat them again.

If the operation has been performed successfully, the work will present a very fine gold surface of a bright deep yellow colour, and is made more *dead* by a longer duration of the periods for colouring, and a still brighter surface may be secured by shortening the periods. It will produce a good colour from four to seven minutes, varying in tint in proportion to the time occupied in the process.

The longer the time occupied in colouring, the deeper and more lasting is the colour upon the work. With the shortest period it is only a mere film of pure gold, of course, but nevertheless it is both rich and beautiful looking. This mixture can with perfect safety be used in proportion to the quantity of work to be coloured, and in the above form of colour I have found many advantages present themselves, irrespective of the advantage in point of economy, in not taking so much off the work to be coloured, or, in other words, in not reducing the weight so much as most mixtures do.

The mixture is easy to prepare, and therefore not so likely to burn, which, when it happens, considerably impairs the colour and finish of the work. It can be employed by an unskilful person if the directions here laid down are attended to. There is no fear of sweating the work, as the colour is a weak one, and at the same time acts quickly.

In colouring jobs and single articles the old colour should be taken for that purpose, and if in a dry state add one ounce of acid and three ounces of water; if liquid, make no addition; and in nearly every instance the colour will be rich and beautiful.

CHAPTER VII.

The Melting and Casting of Gold.

WE have often been consulted in reference to a special branch of the subject we are considering, a branch in which there is very little literature to be procured for safe guidance, viz., the casting of small objects, such as a wedding, keeper, or signet ring, or other odds and ends.

The best way to begin in casting small quantities of gold, or silver, into various objects will be by getting two level pieces of stick charcoal and rubbing the best side of each down quite flat on a stone. A piece of pumice stone will answer this purpose admirably, or an old file may be used instead, if preferred. One of the pieces of charcoal should be longer than the other, and towards the end of this piece, just past the point where the other extends to, should be hollowed out a cup-like cavity for holding the gold or silver while melting it. If it is desired to melt a strip of gold out of a few odd scraps of other articles, suitable for a keeper, wedding, or bangle ring, for this purpose procure a thin piece of iron, about the thickness of a shilling, and cut off a narrow strip, and this, when bent into the proper shape, will form the ingot mould. It will depend on what the casting is to be as to its shape. If, as we have said, it is to be a ring, the strip of iron will want bending into the shape the ring is required.

The proper width is of more importance than the length, because it is as well not to quite fill the mould; bend up the strip of iron to the width you require the ring, and extend the mouth of it out- wards, so as to allow the melted gold or silver to easily run in, and thus prevent spilling. To make a good casting, we repeat again, the size and thick- ness of the iron rim should be in proportion to the article required to be made. The edges of the iron ingot must be made flat with a file, so that it will lie flat between the two pieces of charcoal.

Before fitting the iron ingot between the pieces of charcoal, take a small point, or the blade of a knife, and with it make a few scratches across the charcoals to form air lines; otherwise the metal would spit up out of the mouth of the mould, and cause great loss of material when poured in.

The way the iron ingot is fitted between the two pieces of charcoal is as follows :—Firstly, place it on the longest piece of charcoal, and in which the cavity has been made, with its widened end close up to the cavity. Then place the other piece of charcoal on the top, and bind them together with stout binding wire.

The mitreing of the pieces together should be perfectly true, that if, in looking down the ingot from the mouth, no light is seen, it is right; if, on the contrary, light is visible, the ingot is not perfect, and will not hold the metal when poured into it. A little wet whitening, however, applied to the place and dried will prevent that. Now the mould is made perfect it is ready for receiving the metal desired to cast, and all you have to do is to put the gold into the cavity or cup formed in the longest piece of charcoal, and blow a jet of gas from a mouth blow-pipe on to the gold until it melts.

When the gold has melted, gently tilt the ingot mouth upwards, and the melted gold will at once run into the mould prepared for its reception. It will be necessary to add a little powdered borax to the gold whilst melting, in order to promote its fusion, and prevent the possibility of forming a dry alloy.

The gold, having now been cast into the ingot, should be allowed to rest a little time before separating the two pieces of charcoal, in order to solidify ; when this is done, the casting will be found of the same shape as the inside of the iron rim already described.

The tilting of the molten metal into the ingot should be carefully and slowly done, for if you were to do it quickly, it is very probable the gold or some portion of it would be thrown back again, in consequence of cold air in the ingot, and the gently pouring in would dispel this, by forcing it through the air-holes made across the pieces of charcoal for that purpose. A little practice is required in doing this properly, and it is at all times as well, when inexperience on the part of the workman is a feature of the case, to operate a few times with some inferior metal, and when having acquired the proper knowledge, then proceed to the melting and casting of the gold.

The strip of gold having now been cast, if it is required for a wedding ring, or any plain half-round ring, all you have to do to form it into shape is to hammer it into half-round wire in the groove of a piece of iron or steel, filed into that shape for the purpose.

The groove should be smoothed, firstly with a fine file, and afterwards with a stick of wood and emery powder, before hammering in the gold; otherwise the marks of the file would be transferred to the gold. The smoother and nicer the groove, the better and truer is the form of half-round produced from it, and the less waste occurs by subsequent filing. Thus you save time and trouble. When you have hammered the gold into the above shape it will want annealing, that is, heating it red-hot on a piece of pumice, or some other similar substitute, and when cold, measure the length required, turn it up into the form of a circle, see that the ends mitre nicely and evenly; then solder with gold solder, if you do not want the joint to show afterwards.

When this is effected, you must make the ring round by tapping it with a wooden mallet on a ring triblet; then file up the soldered part to the same evenness as the other part of the ring, and finish off by polishing; the ring is then ready for either gilding or colouring. Its adaptability to which of these processes it shall be submitted can only be decided by a knowledge of the actual fineness of the metal composing the ring under manipulation.

This kind of casting is simple enough in comparison to more intricate work, which is cast in a different manner to that now under consideration. Ordinary plain casting can also be very effectually accomplished without the iron rim, by simply using two pieces of wood charcoal only, and shaping the form of article required to be cast in the pieces of charcoal. This is done by means of a tool suitable for the purpose, a file or knife being sometimes used, but it chiefly depends what kind of article is to be produced as regards the tools required. Scuttlefish is coming very much into fashion for small casting purposes. It is advisable to use it in conjunction with a piece of charcoal, the piece of charcoal having the cavity cut into it for holding the metal to be melted. The impression is made in the scuttlefish by pressure, cutting out with suitable tools, and again pressing in the model of object to be cast, and this is repeated until a perfect mould is obtained, when the metal is cast into it, in the manner described.

Plaster-of-Paris is used for casting purposes, and this also requires a certain amount of practical knowledge to accomplish successful results. The chief feature being to well dry the mould before using, and this must be done very gradually, and therefore takes some time to do it properly; if it is too quickly dried it is liable to chip, and thus the mould would become destroyed. The material is mixed with water into a thick consistency, allowed to set a little, the pattern of object to be cast pressed into it, and then, as before stated, very slowly and gradually dried before using.

Of course, this method of casting is only resorted to for odd articles, such as often happen in a jobbing jeweller's trade, and not in manufacturing on a large scale. Wedding-ring makers cast their bars in the usual manner known to jewellers, rolling and slitting them into wire, and subsequently again rolling in grooves the shape required, and then drawing through draw-plates with holes in them of the shape of wedding rings, and which leaves the wire of the desired form and shape.

Another system of casting is by pouring the molten metal into a mould made of sand, enclosed in a proper receptacle or ingot for that purpose. The sand is of a special kind and is best kept for some time before using it. It works all the better by doing this.

A very useful and suitable ingot mould, for the purpose of casting a signet or other similar ring, is prepared as follows: Take a piece of flat iron, or copper will do if about the thickness of a shilling piece, cut it to the width of two inches, and let it be eight inches long, turn it up and solder the two ends together, and then shape it into a square. Then make another one of similar shape, size, and dimension, file down till each part fit evenly together.

Then solder a piece of wire tube on the opposite sides of one of the parts, and a piece of solid wire on the corresponding sides of the other part, so that the wires will fit truly into the tubes of the other, which are made to receive them when completed and fitted together.

Each bent-up piece of metal should be about one and a quarter inch in depth, and will form a most suitable mould for casting such objects as those above named.

To charge the casting frame, or in other words to make the mould, a quantity of sand is taken and slightly wetted with stale ale, or a solution of potash, and having fitted the ingot together, it is filled from the top, pressed down well, again filled up, and further pressed until a solid compact mass has been formed.

The two parts of the ingot are then separated, and the surfaces which have been severed asunder smoothed, then dusted with fine charcoal secured in a fine muslin cloth or bag. The model of article to be cast is then taken, and laid on the top of the charcoaled sand contained in the lower part of the ingot, which should now be resting on a level board; the other part of the ingot is then fitted on the top and the sand well pressed downwards. This will leave the impression of the articles to be cast on the sand, half of it showing itself on each side of the ingot when taken asunder for the purpose of removing the model previous to the operation of casting.

It is as well to have more depression in the lower part of ingot than equal in each, as better results are accomplished when this is the case. It is necessary to have on one of the sides of the ingot mould a hole for the purpose of receiving the molten metal. This should be on the opposite side to where the fastenings are soldered on. The hole in the metal is best made with a half-round file, and a part of it should be on each side of the separate pieces which constitute the ingot, and the sand is scooped out up to the impression which has been made by the model.

A few scratches should now be made across the sand from the edges of the prepared mould, taking care not to interfere with the mould. These are made for the purpose of letting out the cold air when the molten metal is poured in, for without these precautions are taken, the metal would be forced back again and fly about, a portion of which would be lost and a very imperfect casting produced. The mould should be very carefully dried before using, or the same difficulties will beset the operator.

In making plaster-of-Paris moulds, charcoal should be dusted on the surface as a facing before pressing on the model of the object to be cast, otherwise it would stick, and as a consequence pull out pieces of plaster along with it, and so destroy the perfect symmetry of the moulding, which is everything in the production of a good casting.

Natural objects are oftentimes cast by a process known as "burning out." The natural object is imbedded in pure clay, slowly dried, and afterwards heated nearly red-hot, allowed to cool, when the ashes are blown out with bellows, a hole being left for that purpose, and into which the molten metal is afterwards poured. The clay mould should be heated before pouring in the fused gold or other metal of which the casting is to be composed, for the reasons already made manifest.

For large work casting, frames are made in two halves, that is, they part in the middle, and are prepared by workmen specially kept for that purpose, and are therefore thoroughly trained to the work.

A most important feature in the case of fine casting is to prepare a mould with a fine face ; heat it slowly until thoroughly hot, so that the metal will not spit up in running it in, and with necessary care and experience to guide the operator in his work, perfect results will be produced.

CHAPTER VIII.

Electro Gilding.

THE art of electro-gilding is not generally practised in gold-working establishments, and it is for this reason that we propose giving a few practical directions whereby that art may be successfully accomplished. Electro-gilding is performed by the aid of electricity, whereas gold colouring, in its more practical sense, is more chemical than otherwise. The former is the depositing of one metal upon another, usually of a superior fineness, in order to put a finish on the work and give it a much richer appearance, whilst gold colouring is the removal from the surface of the inferior metals which go to make up the article and leave behind the pure gold.

To successfully perform this task the gold in the alloy should always predominate; in electro-gilding the quality of gold and quantity of alloy is immaterial. The depositing of one metal upon another is a subject of much interest, and different names are given it in accordance with the metal employed, but as we are only concerned at present with gold, the contribution forming the present chapter will be termed gilding.

Electro-gilding may be done either by the aid of heat or in the cold. The work of the jeweller is commonly done with hot baths, they having the advantage of requiring less current strength from the battery, and a solution not so rich in gold, besides producing a colour of very much higher tint than would be the case with a cold bath.

A particular point to be considered, and one that should be always kept well in view in electro-gilding, is to see that the two metals perfectly adhere, for if this is not the case the gold will peel off in the subsequent finishing process. For this purpose the articles should be chemically clean before putting into the bath, and means should be taken to prevent any film of air, or oxide, remaining on them.

Electro-gilding is remarkably simple and easy to accomplish, if the main principles are understood and adhered to. We shall not enter into an elaborate history of the subject of electro-metallurgy, but content ourselves with supplying the necessary practical formulas to enable the manufacturing goldsmith to accomplish his own gilding in his own workshop if he be so disposed. The first thing to be considered will be the source from which the electricity—so necessary for the purpose—is to be derived.

In gilding small objects, and when not required to be in continual use, there is no better generator of electricity for this purpose than the galvanic battery. The one that we prefer is the Bunsen for depositing gold it is simple and very effective when required at irregular intervals, and is therefore most suitable for the manufacturing jewellers and goldsmiths.

It is a small apparatus, and thus takes up little room in the workshop, consisting of a high but narrow cylindrical stoneware jar, for the outer cell, capable of holding two quarts of acid and water; inside this jar or cell is placed a cylinder of zinc of about one-eighth of an inch in thickness, and a copper wire secured to it by means of a binding screw; a porous cell is then placed in the centre of the zinc, and a bar or rod of carbon is put into it, with another piece of copper wire fitted to it.

These two wires of copper serve as conductors of electricity from the battery to the gold solution and from the gold solution to the battery again. The connections of these wires should at all times be perfect, otherwise deposition does not properly take place, and a part of the current is lost, and the gilding will be of too pale a colour.

A leaden collar may be fitted round the top of the carbon rod and the binding screw attached to it for the better prevention of the acid in the cell corroding the connections, and it should then be well coated with melted paraffine wax as a further protection.

The binding screw attached to the zinc should also be well coated with this composition for the same purpose. Having now completed the battery ready for charging, that is, putting in the exciting fluid, into the outer cell, or that which contains the zinc, is put a mixture of oil of vitriol and water, in the proportion of 1 of acid to 40 of water; we have found this strength ample, and with it the zinc lasts much longer, a point of economy not to be lost sight of.

Into the porous cell, or that which contains the carbon element, is put equal parts of oil of vitriol and water, to which is then added 1 oz. of nitric acid; this is our own way of charging, and we prefer it to all others, as it does not give off such fumes as does nitric acid alone, the common way of charging the carbon cell, and by these means it lasts a long time on one charge, it being only necessary to add a small quantity of nitric

G

acid occasionally to the ingredients in the cell to keep up the full current.

The zinc should be amalgamated or coated with mercury. It is done as follows : Put mercury into a coarse flannel bag and repeatedly dip it into muriatic acid after each application to the surface of the zinc; to both inside and outside of the zinc should this process be applied until the zinc presents a bright silvery appearance, when the operation has been carried far enough. Other methods of amalgamation are in vogue for protecting the zinc against the influence of the acid, and we have successfully employed *corrosive sublimate* by adding it to the cell containing the zinc. Nitrate of mercury is also used for this purpose. Having completed all these things the battery is then ready for use.

The zinc element of a battery is called the positive and the carbon the negative pole, on the ground that the zinc engenders the electricity and leaves the cell from the carbon, and through the wire attached to it enters the solution containing the depositing metal ; but in this solution the terms are reversed, for the wire proceeding from the carbon element of the battery, and to the end of which is attached the anode, or plate of gold to be dissolved in the gold solution, becomes the positive, and the wire containing the cathode, or article to be gilt, becomes the negative pole, because the electricity leaves the gold solution by means of this wire and travels back again to the zinc of the battery, and so the circuit continues, unless some obstacle steps in the way and cuts off the current altogether.

Having now amply described the battery by which gilding may be successfully performed, we will proceed at once to describe the most economical and practical solutions to employ along with it.

Electro-gilding is generally done in hot solutions, nevertheless it is sometimes done in cold solutions, more especially is it so with large work, and with this purpose in view we shall commence by giving a solution for cold electro-gilding.

FORMULA No. I.—SOLUTION FOR COLD GILDING.

Fine gold . . . 2½ dwts.
Cyanide of potassium . I ounce.
Water . . . . I quart.

In preparing the solution for use it will be necessary to dissolve the fine gold in *aqua-regia*, in a glass flask with a long neck, heating it over a gas jet or spirit lamp until the gold is all dissolved. The solution thus formed should be evaporated until it becomes of a dark brown and thickly fluid mass, when it should be placed aside to cool. The heating to evaporate the acid may be continued in the flask after complete dissolution has taken place, or otherwise by pouring it into a porcelain dish.

The heating should not be continued too long, or too strongly, for the reason that by so doing the chloride of gold which is now forming, and in which state it is wanted, would be converted into metallic gold again, and therefore become useless for the purposes required. The *aqua-regia* is prepared from a mixture of two parts of hydrochloric acid and one part of nitric acid. It is imperatively necessary that both these acids should be pure, and it is only requisite that the gold in the flask be well covered over with the *aqua-regia* to cause its entire dissolution. For effecting this purpose about two drachms of hydrochloric acid and one drachm of nitric acid will be all that is required to dissolve the above proportion of gold, if the heat is regulated properly.

The chloride of gold having now been prepared in the manner stated, and of course cooled, is dissolved in a pint of water, and a solution of ammonia added to it gradually, and a little at a time, so long as a precipitate continues to be formed. You must avoid adding too much ammonia, how-

ever, under any conditions, or the precipitate, now
called fulminating gold, would be re-dissolved, and
your time and labour wasted.

The strength of the ammonia solution may be in
the proportion of one ounce of ammonia to one
pint of water. Liquid ammonia of the shops may
be used if preferred. The precipitate, after allowing
sufficient time for it to settle to the bottom of the
vessel, is washed with hot water, and then dissolved in a quart of water in which has previously
been dissolved one ounce of cyanide of potassium.
If possible the solution should now be boiled in
order to dispel the odour of ammonia, which is
caused in its connection with cyanide, and the loss
of water by evaporation is then made up, and when
cold it is ready for use.

The quantity of cyanide given in this formula
may be increased or diminished, in accordance with
the intensity of the current used for gilding. With
a weaker current more cyanide is required than
when a more powerful one is employed, and better
results are oftentimes accomplished in this manner
than when a current of too high intensity is used.

To those persons not experienced in dissolving
pure gold for the purpose of making their gold
solutions, it may be more convenient to use pure
chloride of gold already prepared and sold by a

few chemists for the purposes herein described. About 5 dwts. of this chloride of gold would be required to form a solution of the strength above given. Gold precipitated with ammonia forms fulminating gold, a highly explosive compound, if allowed to become dry; it should therefore be immediately made up into solution, after precipitation and washing.

Gold solutions have been made of various proportions of gold to the quart of water, in some cases as much as 10 dwts. has been used, but we have invariably found the proportions we have given have proved ample for all ordinary purposes.

FORMULA No. 2.—SOLUTION FOR COLD GILDING.

Fine gold . . .	2½ dwts.
Cyanide of potassium .	1 ounce.
Water	1 quart.

Dissolve the gold in *aqua-regia*, as before recommended, and evaporate to crystallisation; when cool dissolve in a pint of water and precipitate with a solution of cyanide of potassium—one ounce to the pint; be careful and not add too much, or the precipitate will become re-dissolved. The precipitate is well washed with several waters, and the cyanide in a quart of water is then added to it, the whole boiled for a short time, the lost water made up, and when cold it is ready to receive the work it is desired to gild.

It is advisable to work with as small a quantity of cyanide of potassium as is consistent with economy and efficiency, as too large a proportion only tends to produce deposits of a dirty looking and sandy pale colour. Cold electro-gilding requires a current of more power than is the case with hot gilding, and is not so uniform in its results. Nevertheless it is a great requisition when large articles are to be operated upon, and when the solutions are required too large to be conveniently heated.

FORMULA NO. 3.—SOLUTION FOR HOT GILDING.

Fine gold	.	.	. 18 grs.
Cyanide of potassium	.	10 dwts.
Water.	.	.	. 1 quart.

This solution is prepared after the manner described for formula 1 ; the gold is taken and dissolved in *aqua regia* and evaporated down to an oily looking mass, then dissolved in water and precipitated with ammonia as fulminating gold, the precipitate well washed, and afterwards dissolved in a quart of water containing the cyanide of potassium, heating it until the smell of ammonia has entirely disappeared, and making up the quantity with water to 1 quart again. The temperature at which the solution acts best is 150° to 160° Fahr.

This solution produces a beautiful deep rich gilding with one quart cell of a Bunsen battery by using a fair sized gold anode with which to supply the solution with gold as it is taken up by the articles to be gilt. The quantity of cyanide is always in proportion to its purity and strength; sometimes with us it has required as much as 1 oz. to properly work this solution, therefore always use the best cyanide procurable.

FORMULA No. 4.—SOLUTION FOR HOT GILDING.

Fine gold .   .   . 18 grs.
Cyanide of potassium . 10 dwts.
Water.   .   .   . 1 quart.

Prepare this solution in exactly the same manner as before, with the exception that a solution of cyanide of potassium is employed in precipitating the aqueous chloride of gold, and when well washed the water and cyanide above given are added until a clear solution is formed, the bath is then completed and ready for receiving the work.

Sometimes the electric current is made use of for the purpose of preparing a gold solution, and as many gilders adopt this plan, it will be as well perhaps if we explain the *modus operandi*. It is as follows :

A quart of distilled water, or water which has been boiled and allowed to cool again, is taken and put into an enamelled vessel and placed over a gas jet ; in the centre of the enamelled vessel is placed a porous cell for the purpose of assisting the current back again to the generator or battery.

In the enamelled vessel, which should be capable of holding 1 quart of water or a little more, is dissolved 1 oz. of cyanide of potassium. The porous cell is filled with this solution to the same height as the outer vessel. The battery having been fitted up for working, to the wire issuing from the carbon element is secured a plate of thin rolled gold and placed in the water vessel, and a small piece of copper is attached to the wire issuing from the zinc element and placed within the porous cell ; the current is continued until from 12 to 18 grs. of gold have become dissolved from the gold plate or anode, when it is discontinued and the contents in the porous cell thrown into the receptacle kept for waste waters.

The porous cell is washed and placed aside until again required. The solution may then be used for gilding without further trouble, it being only necessary to hang the articles to be gilt on the wire, previously dipping into the porous cell. The porous cell may be dispensed with altogether in making the gold solution, and a small strip of platinum attached to the zinc wire of the battery, just letting it dip into the cyanide solution, and when it begins to receive a good deposit of gold sufficient will have become dissolved to form a good depositing solution. The solution would then consist of about the following :

FORMULA No. 5.—SOLUTION FOR HOT GILDING.

Fine gold   .   .   . 12 grs.
Cyanide of potassium .   1 oz.
Water .   .   .   . 1 quart.

The amount of gold dissolved during electrical action may be conveniently ascertained by weighing the plate of gold before and after the operation.

This method of preparing the gold bath is a very simple one, and it excludes the possible loss of gold which sometimes occurs in making solutions by the chemical methods, but the gilding produced from chemically made baths is much richer and deeper than those made by means of the battery. By purchasing commercially pure chloride of gold there is not likely to be any great loss, as the dissolving of the gold and subsequent evaporation is dispensed with, and it is here where the loss is most likely to take place. We have produced very satisfactory results with the solution given as formula No. 5.

It is necessary to the constant production of good gilding to maintain as far as possible the gold strength of the solution, otherwise if the solution should become exhausted of its gold the gilding would be of a dirty colour, and not at all saleable; even when they become partly exhausted, the colour is very indifferent. The only way to maintain the proper strength is to have just sufficient cyanide in the bath, combined with enough intensity of current to dissolve from the gold anode a corresponding amount to that deposited upon the articles under its action.

To do this accurately requires a large amount of practical skill and knowledge of the subject, and that can only be acquired by considerable practical experience, without which no amount of book learning will accomplish it satisfactorily.

Gold solutions are frequently strengthened when they become partly exhausted by the addition of chloride of gold, or fulminating gold dissolved in cyanide of potassium, or, on the other hand, by means of the battery in the manner just described. All these processes are troublesome to prepare, however, and we prefer to keep sufficient cyanide

of potassium in the solution to keep up its strength
without any extraneous aid in every case possible.

By the action of the air, and also through the
heating of gold solutions, cyanide of potassium is
converted into carbonate of potassium, and it is
absolutely necessary, therefore, to continually make
small additions of cyanide to the solution to keep it
in proper working order.

A method adopted in gilding chains and other
articles manufactured from common metal, and in
imitation of genuine gold articles, is the following :—

A bath is prepared by dissolving a quantity of
pure gold and making a solution of it in the usual
manner, and then using a large *copper anode* instead
of a gold one in the process of gilding. On the
large scale as much as 1 oz. of fine gold is taken
and treated in this manner.

The articles are gilt until they stand the nitric
acid test, when they are well burnished until they
present a bright gold-like appearance. If the
articles are slightly gilt as a first process and then
burnished, and afterwards more thickly gilt and
again burnished, much less gold is required than
if the process was conducted straight through to
the end without any intermediate burnishing. The
burnishing stops up all the pores of the metal by

the adoption of this plan, and more quickly renders the articles gilt acid proof, and that at the
expense of much less gold being expended on
them. When the solution begins to gild of an inferior colour it is abandoned and another one
made. It produces a surface alloy of about 16 or
18 carat, and well answers the purpose for which
it has been designed.

A gold solution can also be made thus:—Take
fine gold, or standard coin gold will do if the other
is not readily procured, and dissolve it in nitro-
muriatic acid—*aqua regia*—then dilute it with about
3 ozs. of water; this quantity would be to the acid
proportions in which 2 dwts. of gold had been dissolved. When this addition is made to the acid gold
solution it should be neutralized with bi-carbonate
of soda; the point of neutralization is readily ascertained when all effervescence ceases; add 1 pint
of water to this mixture, and afterwards pour it into
another vessel of water in which 3 oz. of the purest
cyanide of potassium and 2 quarts of water which
has been boiled and allowed to cool again are contained.

The ingredients required to make a quart of
this solution would be as follows:—Fine gold for
chloride, 1 dwt.; nitro-muriatic acid, 2 drachms for
dissolving the gold; bi-carbonate of soda, 5 dwts.

for neutralizing the acid in which the gold is dissolved; cyanide of potassium, $1\frac{1}{2}$ oz.; and water, 1 quart. This solution is simply prepared, and there is not much likelihood of losing any of the gold in its preparation if performed by an unskilful operator as there is with some other mixtures. We, however, do not like its working qualities as well as those we have previously given.

The French system of gilding is rather different to our own, and we prefer giving now a few particulars regarding the methods practised. One or two mixtures only will be produced as sufficient illustration of the mode of working.

No. 1.—French Gilding Solution.

Crystallized phosphate of soda . . .	$2\frac{1}{2}$	oz.
Bi-sulphate of soda	10	dwts.
Cyanide of potassium	1	dwt.
Fine gold for chloride	1	dwt.
Water	1	quart.

Dissolve the gold in *aqua regia* and evaporate to crystallization, being careful not to heat it too much and cause its return to the metallic state. Dissolve the phosphate of soda in $1\frac{1}{2}$ pints of the water by the aid of stirring and allow to cool. Dissolve the cyanide and the bi-sulphate of soda in $\frac{1}{4}$ of a pint of water. Dissolve the chloride of gold in the re-

maining ¼ of a pint of the water and pour it slowly
into the cold solution of phosphate of soda, and then
add the solution of bi-sulphate of soda and cyanide
of potassium. The bath is then ready for use after
it has been boiled a short time and the water of
evaporation replaced; it is then a clear solution,
and is worked with a *platinum* anode.

It requires an intense electric current to deposit
from this solution. Two cells of the Bunsen battery, coupled for tension, each holding two quarts,
is fully necessary to successfully operate with this
solution. The bath soon becomes exhausted of its
gold when in use, in consequence of there being
nothing to supply the solution with gold in place
of that taken from it by the articles submitted for
gilding; the platinum anode being insoluble, and
if it were not, is of the wrong colour to that required. The bath, therefore, has constantly to be
replenished with gold to keep it in working condition, and this is done by adding equal parts of
gold ammonium and cyanide of potassium.

This is commonly called *aurate of ammonia*, and
a convenient way of preparing it is after the
following manner:— Transform the gold into a
precipitate of gold ammonium, or aurate of gold,
by precipitating it with spirits of ammonia, or ammonia dissolved in water. Place this substance in

water in the proportion of 2 pints of water to 4 ozs.
of gold, then add cyanide of potassium until the
liquid becomes colourless, and in this form it is
added to the gilding solution just before gilding;
it produces a fine gilding, and should be added to
the solution in proportion to the amount of work
that has been gilt.

In the small way, such as happens to take place
in a manufacturing jeweller's workshop, about 2
drachms of this replenishing mixture added every
day to the gold solution will be found sufficient
for the purpose. In gilding with this solution the
fact must not be overlooked that it requires an intense current, for if so, failure will be the result of
the operator's labours.

No. 2.—French Gilding Solution.

Phosphate of soda	2	ozs.
Bi-sulphate of soda	10	dwts.
Bi-carbonate of soda	5	dwts.
Caustic potash	5	dwts.
Cyanide of potassium	1½	dwts.
Fine gold for chloride	1½	dwts.
Water	1	quart.

All these ingredients may be dissolved together
with the exception of the chloride of gold. The
mixture is better if filtered before adding the gold
chloride. It produces a very fine gilding, and re-

quires powerful electromotive force to work it.   Its
preparation is very simple, but we prefer the
recipes given in the earlier part of the work for
use in our own workshop. A platinum anode is
used in gilding with this solution, and the exhausted
gold is replaced by small additions to the bath of
chloride of gold and the other ingredients. A
quantity of chloride of gold may always be kept
ready for adding to the bath by dissolving it in a
pint of water with a corresponding proportion of
the other salts added to it, and kept in a stoppered
bottle ready at any time.   About 1 oz. of this mixture should be added daily to the bath, or otherwise, in proportion to the amount of work daily
performed. Add the mixture just before gilding.

H

CHAPTER IX.

Some other Modes of Gilding.

THERE are other modes by which gilding can be accomplished than by means of the battery and other electrical appliances, such as simple dipping, that is, immersing in a boiling chemical solution in which gold forms one of the ingredients; contact gilding, or immersion in a gold solution with a more positive metal which causes the solution to give up its gold; paste gilding, or the rubbing the surface of the wares to be gilt with a thick paste composed of neutral salts in which is contained a little gold; and numerous other methods have been practised in treating for the production of those high effects which gold only of all the metals is known to give. But as the inclusion of all would be too comprehensive for a small treatise like this, only those will be given likely to prove of some service to our working metallurgists. To begin with what is known as contact gilding we should proceed thus :—

FORMULA FOR CONTACT GILDING.

Yellow prussiate of potash . . .	2 ozs.
Carbonate of potash	1 oz.
Common salt	1½ ozs.
Pure gold for chloride	2 dwts.
Water	1 quart.

The gold is first of all transformed into chloride in the usual manner. In preparing the mixture for gilding, boil the water, which may conveniently be done by putting it into an enamelled saucepan or other similar vessel; when boiling, add the salts, with the exception of the gold, one after the other, and permit them to boil for two or three minutes, carefully stirring them with a glass rod; then add the solution of chloride of gold slowly to the boiling liquid while continuing the stirring with the glass rod, and permit to boil for two or three minutes longer, after which process the liquid is allowed to cool, and then bottled for future use. The bottle should be provided with a well-ground stopper which materially assists in its preservation.

When required for use take a little of the liquid and heat it to nearly the boiling point, then immerse the article to be gilt in contact with a clean and bright piece of zinc, and gold deposition will immediately take place upon the article, and also upon the zinc, which should be preserved and the

gold recovered by the means presently to be re-
lated.

Gold deposition will also take place in this
solution when cold, but then it takes a little longer
to do it, and the film of gold is very thin; so also in
fact is it with the hot solution, for as soon as the
more positive metal becomes coated with gold,
deposition ceases altogether. The solution can
therefore only be used for very thin deposits of
gold. Ordinary cyanide solutions will deposit
gold on electro-positive metals in the manner here
stated.

Here is another mixture capable of depositing
gold by the simple immersion process, and it has
the reputation of being able to colour 9-carat gold.
It is thus prepared :—

Phosphate of soda	2½ ozs.
Concentrated prussic acid . . .	10 dwts.
Chloride of gold	5 dwts.
Water	1 quart.

The phosphate of soda is firstly dissolved in 1¾
pints of the water, and the prussic acid is then
added; secondly, the chloride of gold is dissolved
in the remaining ¼ of a pint of the water, and then
added to the other solution; and for using it is
heated to about 150° Fahr. The work is, before
dipping in this solution, plunged into a prepara-

tion of mercury, and the adoption of this plan causes it to take the gold much better, by presenting a more positive surface to the work. The following is a good mixture for that purpose :—

Nitrate of mercury	.	.	.	.	.	3 dwts.
Sulphuric acid	.	.	.	.	.	2 drachms.
Water	.	.	.	.	.	.	1 quart.

The layer of mercury caused by immersion in this bath, when dipped in the gold one, is replaced by a gold one of a fine rich appearance. If not sufficiently bright the first dip, the process is repeated by re-dipping in the mercury bath, and afterwards in the gold one again until the desired colour is obtained. Sometimes it is advisable to slightly heat the work after the dipping, when this can be done without injury, and it oftentimes much improves the surface by dispelling the mercury. It is then finished by any one of the modes appertaining to that process.

The assistance of the current may of course be brought into use in all these solutions, the mercury one included, if prepared from cyanide of mercury in cyanide of potassium, the mercury being afterwards evaporated over a clear coke fire, and the articles scratch-brushed, burnished, or polished.

A method of gilding having in combination the

principle of fire-gilding with that of electro-gilding, is performed according to the manner here
directed :—

FORMULA OF ELECTRO-FIRE GILDING.

Cyanide of potassium . .	$1\frac{1}{2}$ ozs.
Cyanide of mercury . . .	4 dwts.
Fine gold for chloride . .	2 dwts.
Water	1 quart.

The articles are gilt by means of a strong current
from two 2 quart cells of a Bunsen's battery,
coupled for tension, and when sufficiently gilded,
the mercury is evaporated by heat and the gold
left behind strong and durable. The usual modes
of finishing are now applied and the operation is
rendered complete.

Grecian Gilding.

This kind of gilding is performed by taking equal
parts of bi-chloride of mercury and chloride of
ammonia and dissolving them in nitric acid to
make a liquid substance, to which is then added
a small portion of gold salt, usually the chloride,
and the whole diluted with a little water, when it
is ready for use. It is generally prepared for
gilding silver wares, and you have only to brush
them over with the composition, which turns them

black, but on exposure to heat in order to expel
the mercury, they assume the appearance of fine
gold of a dull appearance which is made bright by
burnishing.

Gilding by Friction.

This process of gilding is commonly termed *paste
gilding*, and is done by means of a rag, or a cork,
or otherwise by using the thumb, in its application
to the work which is to be gilt. It is chiefly employed upon copper or brass articles that cannot
well be gilt all over, such as the rims to compass
seals, and similar wares, for which purpose it
answers admirably.

The following is the mode of its preparation :—
Dissolve 2 dwts. of chloride of gold, and 1 dwt. of
saltpetre, in as little water as possible. Fine linen
rags are dipped in this solution until the whole is
soaked up, and the rags having thus become
saturated with gold, are allowed to gently dry, then
burned carefully and slowly to a tinder, so as not
to cause loss of gold.

The substance is then reduced to a fine powder
in a mortar, and the article to be gilt, which should
be well polished and free from grease, is rubbed
gently over with the powder by means of a cork
moistened with a solution of salt and water, when

the gold will appear upon the article in its true colour. It has only then to be polished up to give it lustre, with a very small quantity of rouge, by means of a piece of clean wash-leather, and the operation is finished.

SOLUTION FOR GILDING IRON OR STEEL.

Saltpetre	8 ozs.
Common salt	8 ozs.
Alum	4 ozs.
Pure gold	5 dwts.
Water	5 ozs.

Reduce the saltpetre, alum, and salt, to a fine powder and well mix. Dissolve 5 dwts. of thinly rolled gold in *aqua regia* about 1 oz. and evaporate so as to form chloride of gold, and when this is done, add it to the other mixture, and it will be only necessary to dip in the iron or steel to enable either to become immediately gilt. The mixture acts best by heating.

By means of the above solution 9-carat gold can be pot-coloured after the manner of the higher qualities, by using the present fashionable *red-gold alloys* in making up the articles, and using high quality solder in their manufacture. This is a secret not generally known, if at all, in the trade, and we have no doubt, some good commercial successes will eventually be derived from the hint here given, by those persons who hitherto have striven fruitlessly to accomplish such results. It is not necessary to evaporate the *aqua regia* in which the gold has been dissolved in performing the latter operations, as that mixture acts much more quickly by adding it to the other ingredients in its liquid state.

CHAPTER X.

Practical Manipulations.

BEFORE entering upon other matters connected with the art of the goldsmith and jeweller, it is imperatively necessary to impress the fact that absolute cleanliness is an essential element in all operations relating to the foregoing processes, as one of the greatest drawbacks to success is an unclean surface of the articles to be gilt, grease, especially, being very detrimental. The objects to be gilt, therefore, should be carefully cleaned of all fatty matters and dirt, or else the solutions will not act uniformly, and the grease would spread over the entire objects when they came to be scratch-brushed. There are various processes in use for cleaning, in accordance with the particular class of work and kind of metal of which it is composed.

Gold articles are, after the process of polishing, usually washed out in a hot solution of carbonate of soda, by means of a stiff bristle brush, or, in more obstinate cases of dirt, in a hot solution of caustic soda, or potash, which is much more powerful than the former solution.   Old dirty articles of jewellery, when not soft-soldered, are best prepared for gilding by annealing them and scratch-brushing, when, after rinsing in clean water, they are at once transferred to the bath.

New work, with perfectly plain surfaces, can, after the polishing and washing-out process, if it is to be finished *bright*, be at once placed in the gilding liquid, as a better and glossier surface is subsequently produced, by means of the rouging process, than if the work had been annealed, as it always leaves a boil upon the outside which no acid will effectively remove, and which, in some few cases, is most difficult even to do so by mechanical means.

In many instances the form the surface is finally to present, as regards the various styles of finishing gold, silver, and metal goods, is partly or entirely effected before the gilding process, and as it is not always gold that calls for treatment by the hands of the goldsmith and jeweller, we propose giving some general information with reference to the processes of preparing, frosting, and finishing silver and gilt work, which subject, we believe,

will prove highly interesting to a large portion of
our readers, now that silver and gilt work is so
much in fashion.

A few particulars, then, in this direction, while
being a useful auxiliary to the previous information which has been imparted through the pages
of this treatise, may also be the means of sug-
gesting new ideas with regard to gold. But it
must not be understood for one moment, although
every process and every detail may be here laid
down for the perfect and most complete accomplishment of the art, that the uninitiated, or even
less experienced craftsman, can do the same work,
and achieve such good results, as the more skilful
workman.

Take the case of frosting— some workmen can
accomplish this process on the three metals above-
named by means of the scratch-brush, although
the usual method in most workshops is different
in each case; and it is a very difficult matter
indeed to instil into the minds of some workmen
these simple facts, which are not at all difficult
to accomplish when the mind and the proper
tools are brought into play. A softer metal
requires less pressure on the part of the operator,
and softer tools, and a harder metal just the
reverse, and if these things were kept well in view

it would not be difficult to surmount any obstacle which might be thought to stand in the way.

Metal-work is firstly prepared for gilding by dipping in compound acid solutions, and a frost is easily produced by these means. It is much quicker than the use of the brush, although after gilding it is submitted, in the same manner as silver, to the scratch-brush. But while metal-work is most advantageously frosted by acids, no good possible results can be arrived at with silver, or by its treatment in any analogous manner, as the colour, in the first place—and this is highly important commercially—would be very inferior to that produced by other means, and the frost would not be effected evenly, and thus in no manner compare with that produced by the scratch-brush.

The compound dipping mixtures for metal-goods consist as follows. Each one effects a clean, bright, and frosted surface upon work submitted to their various actions, and this again, of course, is always in proportion to the nature and composition of the alloy of which the work is composed. The action being more energetic in copper zinc alloys, therefore care should be taken that they are not left too long in the dipping mixture, to prevent disastrous results.

No. 1. Dead Dipping Mixture.

Nitric acid	10 ozs.
Sulphuric acid	5 ozs.
Common salt	1 dwt.
Sulphate of zinc	1 dwt.

In preparing this mixture add the sulphuric acid to the nitric, and lastly put in the common salt and sulphate of zinc, in a state of fine powder. In dipping, keep your work free from water, and let it remain in the solution from a few seconds to a few minutes, according to the nature of the work. Before employing this mixture the work must be scrupulously clean, and free from grease of every kind, and this is effected by dipping in the following solution :—

No. 2. Caustic Potash Dipping Mixture.

Caustic potash	2 ozs.
Boiling water	20 ozs.

This solution is used at nearly the boiling point, which frees the articles from dirt and grease, the last traces being removed by using a stiff brush wet with the mixture, at which stage the articles are rinsed in water, dried in sawdust, and are then ready for the deadening mixture dip.

Sometimes wares, previous to gilding, are put through another solution, subsequent to that of dead-dipping, and well rinsing in water to arrest the action of the acid which still clings to the work in minute fragments, after its withdrawal from the bath. It is called the cyanide dip, and its ingredients consist as follows :—

No. 3. CYANIDE DIPPING MIXTURE.

Cyanide of potassium . . . 2 ozs.
Boiling water . . . . 20 ozs.

The cyanide of potassium is dissolved in the hot water, when it is ready for use. It should always be used in a hot state to be effectual.

The frosting of silver is not done with an acid or combination of acids, but is simply due, as already stated, to the effects of the scratch-brush specially provided for that purpose. The scratch-brushes take different forms, according to the kind of work to be submitted to them for frosting. They are made of various strengths; that is, the wires of them are specially prepared of several thicknesses, and when a very fine satin finish is required, a brush of very fine wire is taken, and so on. A brush with wires thicker and thicker in proportion is taken as a more extended roughness is desired. These wire scratch-brushes are fixed upon a horizontal spindle in the lathe; the latter is made to revolve by means of the foot of the operator and a treadle attached to the crank of the lathe, but where a gas-engine can be employed it is far preferable, as the speed is much greater and far more regular.

Frosting requires great speed to do the work nicely. The wires of the scratch-brush must lie even on the surface, all of the same length, and always kept straight at the points, otherwise the frosting will not be regular. Sometimes the little hand scratch-brushes are employed for coarser work; four of them are taken and firmly secured in four corresponding grooves in a circular chuck, which screws into the lathe.

The ends of the four little brushes are repeatedly cut off as occasion requires, in order to present a straight surface for continual contact with the work, without which it would not present a uniform appearance. We have frosted silver in the following mixture :—

DEAD DIPPING MIXTURE FOR SILVER.

Sulphuric acid	.	.	.	1 oz.
Water .	.	.	.	1 oz.
Saltpetre	.	.	.	2 dwts.

The sulphuric acid is added to the water and the saltpetre in a state of fine powder is afterwards put in. It is used in the boiling state and takes a few minutes to accomplish the desired object.

Silver wares are made to present a dead appearance by using very fine emery cloth as a last operation previous to finishing, and when skilfully performed produces a nice effect.

Gold wares can be treated in the same manner for both colouring and gilding, or they may be frosted by the scratch-brush previous to the chemical process, or, on the other hand, well brush with pumice and a hard stiff brush, using just sufficient water to enable the pumice to hold together. Very beautiful effects may be produced by any of these means on either gold or silver goods if done with care and experience.

The colour in electro-gilding is a very important matter, and a few particulars regarding its variation and the conditions under which it changes are worthy of a place here.

For deep gilding the anode or plate of gold should be large, for that at once provides a mode of at once regulating the current strength of the battery and colour of the deposit produced. It can be immersed altogether in the solution and thus gild a deep rich colour, or by immersing a small portion only, quite a pale gold colour will be produced if the objects to be gilt are large in them-

I

selves and required the full size of gold plate to gild them properly. Also by a strong current and large anode quite a deep red gold colour can be produced, and the very opposite with a weak cur-rent and small anode. Beautiful yellow gold is produced between these two extremes.

Gold solutions for gilding are kept in enamelled iron vessels, or of porcelain, placed inside of another vessel that can be heated direct by a gas jet or other means if preferable. Plain articles gild much more readily than intricate work, and with less current strength of battery power. So also does the small electro-positive metals; therefore these particulars should always be looked to in the general treatment of goods that are continually coming under the gilder's notice.

When it is intended to give an article a very thick deposit, it will be advisable to scratch-brush it several times with a solution of size and water or beer and water, between the intermediate coats of gold, and by these means a very durable and lasting casing of gold can and will be put on.

There are other means of producing colour in electro-gilding than by the current and size of anode used, means by which almost any colour can be obtained. In order to obtain red gold it has been recommended to add to the bath a little of the acetate of copper reduced to powder and dissolved in water each evening after the day's work has been done, and to obtain green and white gilding a little powdered nitrate of silver prepared and added in the same way. A dead gilding is produced by adding a little of the fulminate of gold to the bath immediately before gilding.

But a better way than either of these would be as follows : To obtain a beautiful red gold deposit with either of the formulas before given for hot electro-gilding, take from 6 to 9 grs. of cyanide of copper, and dissolve it in just sufficient cyanide of potassium for effecting that purpose and add it to the gold bath, and if the current strength, size of anode, and cyanide in the bath are equal a fine red gold deposit will be at once produced.

Another way of producing red gilding is by using a large copper anode until some signs of a copper colour began to appear when it is at once abandoned and replaced by a large gold one until the surplus copper is removed from the solution, when another exchange may with advantage take place again. But the safest and best way of all is to work the solution with an alloyed gold anode.

To obtain a greenish gilding, take from 3 to 6 grs. of cyanide of silver and add it to the gold bath. The current strength of the battery in order to deposit this colour must be moderate, neither too strong nor too weak. With a weak current too much silver would be deposited, while too strong a one would deposit too much gold to produce the intermediate effects required.

There are various devices for improving the bad colour of gilding when it cannot be produced rich enough looking for commercial purposes, although plenty of gold has been deposited, in fact too much from a pecuniary point of view, and this is brought about through endeavouring to procure the right colour with the solution, and in that way causing more gold to be deposited than is necessary to the proper coating of the work. This result, however, is only caused by the solution working in a defective manner ; perhaps from too much cyanide being in the bath and too little gold.

It is therefore advisable to work with as little cyanide as possible compatible with the efficiency and conductability of the solution. A good mixture for improving bad gilding is composed of equal parts of saltpetre, salammoniac and borax. These ingredients are reduced to powder, mixed with a little water, the surface of the work brushed over with it, then heated on a copper pan until it assumes a dark colour, when it is plunged into a pickle of sulphuric acid and water in the proportion of 1 of acid to 20 of water. When the colouring salts have become dissolved by this mixture the work is removed, rinsed in clean water, and scratch-brushed or burnished, and a fine rich gold colour will be the reward of the operator for his labour. There are other recipes for effecting this end, but this one is as good as any, and may at all times be used with advantage and certainty.

CHAPTER XI.

Mixing Alloys.

ONE of the most important features in gold working establishments is that of preparing the different alloys or standards which are continually being required for use in the manufacture of the various articles peculiar to the several branches of the trade. And as accuracy is an indispensable factor in this matter, nothing but sound and reliable information will be given for the guidance of those who may prefer to adopt this system ; and having given the matter much consideration, both for ourselves, and others who have consulted us, we repeat, that it is a most thoroughly practical and reliable method for improving and reducing any quality of gold to higher or lower standards.

To begin with, if it is desired to reduce 22-carat gold to 18-carat, proceed thus :—

To Reduce 22-carat to 18-carat Gold.

Multiply 20 by the difference in carats between

22-carat and 18-carat, which is 4-carats, and then divide the result by 18, the number of carats and quality required. The result of this will be 4 dwts. 10⅔ grs. of alloy to be added to every ounce of 22-carat gold in order to reduce it to 18-carat gold of standard proportions.

EXAMPLE 1.

20 × 4 = 80 ÷ 18 = 4 dwts. 10⅔ grs. alloy.

Or, on the other hand, you can multiply 20 by 3⅓ dwts. the difference between 22-carat and 18-carat in fine gold, and divide the result by 15 dwts., the amount of fine gold contained in one ounce of 18-carat gold.

EXAMPLE 2.

20 × 3⅓ = 66⅔ ÷ 15 = 4 dwts. 10⅔ grs. alloy.

Or, the difference in the standard may be taken in grains, when fractional parts appear, like the above. Multiply 20 by the grains 80, and divide by the quality required, which in this case must also be reduced to grains, when the actual quantity of alloy required will also appear in dwts. and grs. as before shown.

EXAMPLE 3.

20 × 80 = 1600 ÷ 360 = 4 dwts. 10⅔ grs. alloy.

When 18-carat gold is to be the standard dealt with, the method of calculation and reduction will be the same, but the figures will be different, in accordance with the difference in the quality.

To Reduce 18-carat to 15-carat Gold.

Multiply 20 by the difference in carats, viz., 3, between 15-carat and 18-carat, and divide the result by 15-carat, the quality required. The final result will be 4 dwts. of alloy to be added to each ounce of 18-carat in order to reduce it down to 15-carat standard gold.

Example 1.

20 × 3 = 60 ÷ 15 = 4 dwts. alloy.

Or, again, you can multiply 20 by $2\frac{1}{2}$ dwts., the difference in fine gold between 15 and 18-carat, and divide the result by $12\frac{1}{2}$ dwts., the amount of fine gold 15-carat contains in the above numeral of 20 dwts. The result of this will be 4 dwts., to be added to every ounce of 18-carat scrap, of copper or other alloy, to make 15-carat standard gold.

Example 2.

20 × $2\frac{1}{2}$ = 50 ÷ $12\frac{1}{2}$ = 4 dwts. alloy.

If we reduce this quality on the principle of grains

being the multiplier, it would then appear as
follows :—

EXAMPLE 3.

20 × 60 = 1200 + 300 = 4 dwts. alloy.

This principle can be applied to all the standards
alike, and in fact any quality ascertained by assay
can be so treated, and if carefully calculated, the
result cannot fail to be satisfactory in every degree.

One more example of this principle of reducing
gold alloys will be given to show its application to
any possible mixture. Suppose we have a bar of
metal containing 22, 18, 15, and 13-carat mixed
golds, and by assay it comes out at 8 ozs. 17 dwts.
per lb., fine gold, we proceed thus, if it is required
to make 9-carat standard gold :—

TO REDUCE 8 OZS. 17 DWTS. 0 GRS. TO 9-CARAT GOLD.

8 ozs. 17 dwts. 0 gr. ÷ 12 = 0 oz. 14 dwts. 18 grs.
0 oz. 14 dwts. 18 grs. × 24 = 354 grs.
4 ozs. 10 dwts. 0 gr. ÷ 12 = 0 oz. 7 dwts. 12 grs.
0 oz. 7 dwts. 12 grs. × 24 = 180 grs.
20 × 354 = 7080
20 × 180 = 3600
7080 − 3600 = 3480
3480 ÷ 180 = 19 dwts. 8 grs. alloy.

There will be required to add to each ounce of
this mixed alloy 19 dwts. 8 grs. of copper in order

to make 9-carat standard gold. There are other ways of reducing, very simple in themselves when the standards are level, as the following will prove :—

To Reduce 18-carat to 12-carat Gold.

$$20 \times 18 = 360$$
$$20 \times 12 = 240$$
$$360 - 240 = 120$$
$$120 \div 12 = 10 \text{ dwts. alloy.}$$

To one ounce of 18-carat gold, 10 dwts. of some other alloy is required to make 12-carat gold. If it is desired to form 9-carat gold from pure gold as the starting point, proceed on the same principle as here shown :—

$$20 \times 24 = 480$$
$$20 \times 9 = 180$$
$$480 - 180 = 300$$
$$300 \div 9 = 33\tfrac{1}{3} \text{ dwts. alloy.}$$

To one ounce of fine gold therefore, in order to make 9-carat, there is required to be added 1 oz. 13 dwts. 8 grs. of alloy, making a grand total of 2 oz. 13 dwts. 8 grs.

In this example the 24 represents fine gold, there being that number of carats in an ounce. The 20 as before represents the number of pennyweights in an ounce, and the 9 represents 9 carats, the quality required to be made.

When it is necessary to *improve* the quality, the system to be worked upon is somewhat different to the one here laid down. We will therefore proceed to explain what it is, and in doing so shall treat of the qualities more generally in use.

To Improve 15-carat to 18-carat Gold.

Multiply 20 by the difference short 2½ dwts. and divide the result by 5, the difference between 18-carat and fine gold per ounce.

Example 1.

20 × 2½ = 50 ÷ 5 = 10 dwts. fine gold.

You have therefore to add to every ounce of 15-carat, 10 dwts. of *fine gold*, in order to make 18-carat standard gold.

To Improve 12-carat to 18-carat Gold.

Multiply 20 by the difference short of fine gold between 12 and 18-carat, viz., 5 dwts., and divide by 5 dwts., the difference between 18-carat and fine gold in the ounce, 18-carat being 5 dwts. short of purity, or containing 15 dwts. fine gold per ounce.

Example 2.

20 × 5 = 100 ÷ 5 = 20 dwts. fine gold.

To make this mixture it will be seen, 20 dwts. of fine gold is necessary to make 18-carat of standard proportions.

To Improve 9-carat to 18-carat Gold.

Multiply 20 again by the difference in the fineness between 9 and 18-carat, which is $7\frac{1}{2}$ dwts., and divide by 5 dwts., as usual in making 18-carat gold.

Example 3.

$$20 \times 7\frac{1}{2} = 150 \div 5 = 30 \text{ dwts. fine gold.}$$

To make 18-carat from 9-carat it requires 1 oz. 10 dwts. of fine gold to be added to each ounce of 9-carat it is desired to improve.

In more complicated qualities, the easiest method will be, to reduce to grains the difference short of that required, and multiply them by 20, and then divide by the difference in dwts. between the quality wanted and fine gold per ounce. The result will be in grains.

If the difference in the quality wanted and fine gold per ounce is divided by grains, then the result would be in dwts. and not grains.

When it is desired to improve any quality of gold to a higher standard with gold coins, the following plan would be resorted to :—

TO IMPROVE 15-CARAT TO 18-CARAT WITH COINS.

$$20 \times 15 = 300$$
$$20 \times 18 = 360$$
$$360 - 300 = 60$$
$$60 \div 4 = 15 \text{ dwts. gold coin.}$$

All the calculations previously elucidated can be applied to the mixing with gold coins, the only difference being the division is the number of carats, dwts., or grains, between the quality wanted and 22, whereas with fine gold mixing, it is the number between the quality wanted and fine gold, which is 24.

With silver mixing it is only necessary, if it is desired to raise any quality short of standard up to that standard, to multiply the difference short of standard by 40 and then divide by 3 ; or multiply 20 by 3 and divide by $1\frac{1}{2}$; the result will be the quantity required of fine silver in dwts., for every ounce of the inferior mixture, in order to make standard quality.

For the sake of illustration, suppose the alloy to be treated is, by assay, reported 3 dwts. per ounce worse than standard, we should proceed thus to make it standard :—

$$40 \times 3 = 120 \div 3 = 40 \text{ dwts. fine silver ;}$$
or
$$20 \times 3 = 60 \div 1\frac{1}{2} = 40 \text{ dwts. fine silver.}$$

It will thus be seen we have to add to each ounce
of the previous mixture 2 ounces of fine silver in
order to improve it to standard proportions.

In reducing silver it is only requisite to multiply
20 by the difference short of purity and then
divide by the standard required. For instance, if
a standard of ·800 is wished for, proceed in the
following manner :—

$$20 \times 4 = 80 \div 16 = 5 \text{ dwts. alloy.}$$

To one ounce of fine silver 5 dwts. of alloy is
required to make ·800 standard. If standard silver
were taken for reduction the following would be
the plan :—

$$20 \times 2\tfrac{1}{2} = 50 \div 16 = 3 \text{ dwts. 3 grs. alloy.}$$

The latter quantity of alloy is necessary to add to
the standard of silver of ·925 fineness, in order to
reduce it down to ·800 fineness.

We trust to have now made the matter plain to
all who are interested ; as a quick and accurate
method of preparing alloys of gold and silver is
knowledge gained, and oftentimes valuable time
and labour saved.

CHAPTER XII.

Useful Imitation Alloys.

SEVERAL new alloys have been introduced of late years in imitation of gold and silver, and attempts have been made to use them in the manufacture of imitation jewellery and watch-cases, in place of gold and silver. Some few of these will be reproduced here, for it is as well that the practical jeweller should have some knowledge of the various substitutes that are brought into competition with the genuine precious metals.

In a few instances these substitutes for gold and silver have so close a resemblance to the real articles, that it has been a difficult question to decide the point by the usual tests known to practical jewellers, and thus frauds have been practised in a most extensive manner, without the least thought of suspicion as to the absolute genuineness of the metal being created in the minds of purchasers. Were these alloys to be distinguished by a special mark a very useful purpose would be served by their manufacture, as a cheap metal, honestly used, is at the present time capable of great utility; if it can be manufactured to resist all, or nearly all, external agents, such, for instance, as air and moisture, heat and light, the alkalies and any single acid, a very valuable addition is made to metallurgical art; and there is no knowing to what industrial purposes it might be brought to bear, even outside the jewellery trade. One of these mixtures is prepared as follows :—

	oz.	dwts.	grs.
Fine gold	0	4	4
Pure platinum	0	0	15
Tungstic acid	0	0	6
Pure copper	1	0	0
	1	5	1

This mixture is equal to 5-carat gold in value, but has the appearance of 18-carat coloured alloy. It is named *Aphthit*, or unchangeable. It is melted into bars by taking the copper, platinum, and tungsten, and placing them in a crucible, to which is afterwards added a little fine powdered charcoal to prevent the oxidising influence of the air by protecting the metals. When completely melted the alloy is well stirred, and then granulated by pouring it into a deep vessel containing water, and in which has previously been dissolved a small quantity, in equal proportions, of slaked lime and carbonate of potash, it being claimed for this addition the property of making the granulated alloy much cleaner and tougher.

Having collected and dried the granulated metal, it is again melted along with the gold, and run into ingot moulds, when it is ready for rolling and slitting into wire, for the purpose of being worked into the desired object. The colour of the mixture is varied by changing the proportions of the metals. A much paler colour is shown by increasing the proportions of platinum and reducing those of copper. Various fluxes have been recommended for use in the melting, but all that is required is a little powdered charcoal to prevent the air from acting on and oxidising the alloy, which it rapidly does when exposed to it in the molten state.

Another alloy in which platinum enters into composition with gold, and claims to have nearly the same colour as pure gold ; it is, however, erroneous, as platinum changes the colour of gold sooner than any other known metal, and that also with the smallest possible quantity mixed with it. Lecturers and demonstrators at technical colleges

K

put several other metals before platinum in this respect, but it is all a mistake, and proves a thorough want of practical knowledge as regards the rapid transformation of colour gold undergoes when mixed with this metal. The following is the formula for this alloy :—

	oz.	dwts.	grs.
Fine gold .	1	0	0
Pure platinum . .	0	2	6
	1	2	6

This mixture possesses great density as well as elasticity, and was therefore considered at one time a valuable alloy for dental springs. It has a colour more nearly resembling pale 18-carat gold alloys than the one claimed for it by certain writers.

Another alloy which has been prepared to imitate gold, and claiming to resemble 12-carat gold in colour, is here given :—

	oz.	dwts.	grs.
Pure platinum . ,	0	6	16
Pure copper . .	1	0	0
	1	6	16

This alloy is pale in colour, and not at all like 12-carat prepared of a deep rich colour. It may, to some extent, resemble a very pale 12-carat gold alloy, and that is as close as the two can be brought together in their resemblance to each other.

The old-fashioned platinum alloy, in imitation of the bright gold alloys of thirty years ago, can hardly be said to have any golden tinge in its appearance. It certainly withstood the acid test very well, and this will be the only point of resemblance worthy of comparison. There were two formulas for making up the mixture, as follows :—

No. 1.

	oz.	dwts.	grs.
Pure copper . .	1	0	0
Pure platinum . .	0	8	18
Pure spelter . .	0	1	6
	1	10	0

No. 2.

	oz.	dwts.	grs.
Pure copper . .	1	0	0
Pure platinum . .	0	9	6
Fine silver . .	0	0	18
	1	10	0

The colours of these alloys were white, like the common silver alloys of ·600 standard, and without a tinge of yellow in them. There can be very little doubt but that such alloys were manufactured to imitate the old pale, almost white-looking 9-carat alloys in use nearly half a century ago.

An alloy of gold and platinum which we prepared some years ago for a special purpose was composed of the following :—

GOLD PLATINUM ALLOY.

	oz.	dwts.	grs.
Fine gold . .	1	0	0
Platinum scrap .	1	15	0
Swedish copper wire	4	0	0
Pure spelter . .	0	5	0
	7	0	0

It produced an alloy resembling 9-carat bright in colour, and withstood the test of nitric acid fairly well, but was harder and more difficult to work than a gold alloy of similar colour. It cost about 17s. 6d. per ounce to prepare ready for working.

A new alloy has of late years been sprung upon the market which stands the nitric acid test equal in every respect to 12 or 15-carat gold ; when finished by lapping it presents an appearance quite equal to these qualities. It is called *false gold* or *mystery gold.* The formula for making the compound is this :—

MYSTERY GOLD.

	oz.	dwts.	grs.
Pure copper wire . . .	1	0	0
Clean platinum scrap . .	0	3	18
Pure bar tin	0	3	18
	1	7	12

This compound is very hard and difficult to work. Its cost being about 3s. per ounce. The mixture should be well stirred before pouring, otherwise it will not mix well and become homogeneous.

Another alloy having a gold-like appearance is made up of the undermentioned substances:—

DEEP GOLD-LIKE ALLOY.

	oz.	dwts.	grs.
Swedish copper wire . .	1	0	0
Pure spelter	0	1	9
Charcoal iron . . .	0	0	15
Pure lead	0	0	6
	1	2	6

This alloy is non-oxidisable by ordinary means, retains its colour for a long time, boils out a deep colour resembling 20-carat deep gold. Rolls and works fairly well, but rather more difficult to solder than the ordinary copper zinc alloys; requires no gilding, and when finished by rouging presents a rather taking appearance.

Having given a few of the principal imitation

gold-like alloys, we will give another one before
concluding this part of the subject now under consideration. The formula is :—

IMITATION GOLD ALLOY.

	oz.	dwts.	grs.
Pure copper .	1	0	0
Pure platinum.	0	7	12
Fine silver .	0	3	12
Brass . .	0	7	12
Nickel . .	0	3	12
	2	2	0

This alloy is said to be both malleable and
ductile, takes a high polish, and resembles 18-carat
in colour. This, however, cannot be true, as the
white metals are in far too large quantities for the
deep colour of the mixture to be retained, and our
own opinion is it would be quite as pale as the old
bright gold of a bygone day.

This matter would be incomplete without a reference to some of the mixtures that have been attempted in imitation of silver. An anti-corrosive
alloy has been prepared for making into writing
pens of the following composition :—

	oz.	dwts.	grs.
Pure platinum.	1	0	0
Pure silver .	0	15	0
Pure copper .	0	5	0
	2	0	0

This forms a very hard alloy, elastic, and of a colour between silver and platinum.

Another alloy which has been tried for mirrors, and reported capable of taking a good polish, is made up of the following substances :—

	oz.	dwts.	grs.
Pure copper . .	0	11	15
Pure platinum . .	0	1	21
Pure bar tin . .	0	5	12
Pure spelter . .	0	0	16
Arsenic . . .	0	0	8
	1	0	0

This alloy is white in colour, and while being capable, as stated, of taking a good polish, we are doubtful as to its working capabilities.

An alloy we have prepared in imitation of platinum, capable of taking a very high and lustrous polish and standing the acid test fairly well, was the following :—

	oz.	dwts.	grs.
Pure copper . .	0	10	0
Bar tin . . .	0	5	0
Nickel . . .	0	4	6
Platinum . .	0	0	18
	1	0	0

This alloy retained its colour for a considerable period without tarnishing, but the greatest draw-

back was its unworkable qualities. For objects
that could be cast it answered admirably; for other
manipulations its brittleness practically prevented
its use.

An alloy of silver and platinum, and also one of
silver and gold, have been reproduced from the old
formula formerly used in diamond set work, and it
is now being pushed into the market—under another
name—as a cheap substitute for platinum, to be
used alternately with red 9-carat gold for chain
links, crosses, bracelets, and numerous other wares
manufactured by the jeweller.

For setting work it is claimed to be especially
useful on account of its non-tarnishable qualities,
and also of its spark-like brightness, which latter
characteristic, it is asserted, it always maintains in
effective brilliancy, and at the same time resists
every oxidising influence. But as regards the latter
quality we deny it, for when submitted to us we
very quickly oxidised it, and gave it a coal-black
appearance in the course of a few seconds. The
formula for making it is this:—

	oz.	dwts.	grs.
Fine silver . .	o	18	o
Pure platinum . .	o	2	o
	I	o	o

Another formula is—

	oz.	dwts.	grs.
Fine silver . .	0	18	0
Fine gold . .	0	2	0
	1	0	0

These alloys are easily worked, being both malleable and ductile, and also possessed of tenacity. But as none of these alloys are practically likely to become of great commercial utility in the jewellery trade, further detailed description is unnecessary, and we shall proceed to the next chapter and discuss matters of more general importance.

CHAPTER XIII.

Hints and Helps.

It has been said by some writers that the value of the base metal which is required in the making up of an alloy of a certain standard is taken into consideration in determining the quality of gold by alloy for Hall-marking purposes. Now this idea is erroneous, for every standard should actually contain a fixed amount of fine gold, regardless of the value of alloy contained therein.

In estimating or expressing the fineness of gold the whole quantity spoken of is to be divided into 24 equal parts, and the number of those parts that are fine gold determines the standard or quality. If 18 parts of the 24 are fine gold and 6 parts are of alloy, the quality is 18-carat. If 9 parts of the whole are fine gold and the other 15 base metal, the mass treated is 9-carat fine, and the principle continues through all the range of carats.

The money value of the alloy added to reduce the quality of the gold does not at all enter into the determination of the standard of the work to be assayed, whether it is silver, copper, or any other metal so added ; the number of parts of fine gold only is the correct standard of the mixture, and the alloy, whatever it is, is not taken into account at all.

Gold Testing Needles.

Many of our readers will require to know, by reason of the necessities of their vocation, how to ascertain approximately the value and purity of the various articles of gold occasionally brought under their notice in trade. This can be done by the use of *test needles*, which are to be bought from assayers and material dealers. They consist of ten or twelve, and in some cases more, of little slips of metal, to the ends of which are soldered pieces of gold of known standards, from 7-carat up to 18-carat. With these and a good touchstone—a piece of black basalt—a fairly correct opinion can be formed of the quality of any gold alloy.

The usual nitric acid testing mixture is also employed as an adjunct to these; in the higher qualities *aqua-regia* is used as the test acid because

nitric acid does not act upon gold alloys of those
qualities, and therefore gives no such indications
by change of colour as is to be seen in the lower
qualities.   To operate with the test needles, rub the
article to be tested upon the stone till you have
a clear gold-like stripe of about the width of a
shilling in thickness, then alongside of it rub one
of the testing needles which you suppose to be
about the same in quality, and apply to both at the
same time a drop of the testing acid.   The inferior
quality will change colour firstly, under the action
of the acid, and if very low in quality the streak
will disappear almost immediately.   The process is
continued by trying the needles, higher or lower,
as the case may be, till one is found whose action
is the same under the acid as the alloy being
tried.

A full set of test needles are very useful in
a business where there is often inquiry as to the
quality of gold articles, and with little practice and
experience nearly correct results can at all times be
arrived at.   It is not safe to express an opinion as
to the quality of gold by inspection only, colour
being in that case the principal guide, and in the
present advanced state of preparing alloys of gold
it cannot be depended upon in any way as thoroughly sound and reliable evidence.

New Substitute for Silver.

A new alloy in imitation of sterling silver has been prepared by taking and incorporating together by fusion the undermentioned substances:—

	oz.	dwts.	grs.
Charcoal iron . .	0	13	0
Pure Nickel .	0	4	12
Tungsten .	0	0	12
Aluminum .	0	1	0
Copper . .	0	1	0
	1	0	0

This mixture costs about as much as German silver, and is said to withstand the action of sulphur; is not attacked by organic acids, and only slightly by mineral acids.

Gold Lacquer.

Shellac, 1 oz.; turmeric, 1 oz.; sandarac, 5 dwts.; annatto, 5 dwts.; dragon's blood in powder, 15 grs.; spirit of wine, 1 pint. Shake this mixture at intervals for a couple of days, and then pour off the clear liquor for use. The lacquer should be applied with a large camel-hair brush; warm the article till too hot to hold, and then lacquer quickly; cover every part, and do not go over the same twice. Bright work should be burnished before lacquering.

Recovering Gold and Silver from Plating Solutions.

Boil the solution of gold, which is usually made up of cyanide, in an enamelled iron kettle, to which is added occasionally a small portion of stannate of soda, and the boiling is continued until the gold has combined with the tin and formed a black precipitate. Silvering solutions no longer useful may be treated in exactly the same manner.

Gold-coloured Alloy.

This alloy is said to have a fine grain, very malleable, capable of taking a high polish, and in many respects resembles gold of the highest standards. It is made of—

	oz.	dwts.	grs.
Pure copper . .	1	0	0
Pure grain tin . .	0	3	6
Manganese . .	0	1	3
Bitartrate of potash .	0	1	18
Salammoniac . .	0	0	15
Chalk . . .	0	0	6
	1	7	0

The copper is recommended to be first melted; the manganese, potash, salammoniac, and chalk are successively added in small quantities at a time. The tin is then added, and after fusion, quickly poured and allowed to cool, when it is ready for rolling.

Dead Dipping Mixture.

A good recipe for producing a clear matt or fine dull dead appearance is :—Nitric acid 6 parts, sulphuric acid 2 parts, sulphate of zinc 1 part, water 2 parts. Dip the articles and rinse, again dip and rinse, until the clear matt and colour desired is obtained.

To Distinguish Steel from Iron Tools.

It is difficult to distinguish between iron and steel tools having the same polish and workmanship. Place a drop of dilute nitric acid—four parts of water to one of acid—upon the tool; if it remains clean, it is of iron, while if of steel it will show a black mark where touched with the acid. This is a simple and ready test.

A Soldering Fluid free of Acid.

Take zinc or spelter in small pieces 1 oz., muriatic acid 3 ozs.; when the acid has become saturated with the zinc, which is indicated by the ceasing of the effervescence of the acid, and any remaining portions of the zinc undesolved. The dissolution of the zinc is greatly assisted by gentle heat. Decant the clear solution from any sediment that may remain, and add to the clear liquor 1 oz. of spirits of ammonia, which will neutralise all the free acid, then dilute with about 4 ozs. of water. This mixture will not rust iron or steel, and will answer all the purposes necessary to a soldering fluid.

Hard Solders.

For 18-carat gold, take 18-carat scrap 1 part, silver $\frac{1}{8}$th part, composition $\frac{1}{12}$th part. For 15-carat gold take 15-carat scrap 1 part, silver $\frac{1}{5}$th part, composition $\frac{1}{12}$th part. For 9-carat gold, take 9-carat scrap 1 part, silver $\frac{1}{4}$th part, composition $\frac{1}{6}$th part. For silver, take fine silver 1 part, composition $\frac{1}{3}$ part.

Colouring Mixture for Gilt Work.

Sulphate of copper 1 dwt., acetate of copper 2 dwts., salammoniac 2 dwts., saltpetre 2 dwts., icy acetic acid 1 oz.; mix these ingredients well together, and brush over the articles to be coloured with it, or otherwise dip them into the mixture, and then heat them on a copper pan until quite black. They are afterwards boiled out in a pickle composed of equal parts of oil of vitriol and water, which quickly removes the black coating, and displays a fine gold colour. If the articles are scratched before colouring they will come out of this pickle perfectly bright, when after drying the treatment is terminated.

Instantaneous Silvering Mixture.

Mix 1 part of chloride of silver, 7 parts cream of tartar, and 5 parts of common salt, finely powdered and dried in an oven. When required for use moisten a little with water, and rub it with a piece of fine linen on the object, which should be thoroughly clean. Polish with a piece of wash-leather upon which has been dusted fine chalk or whiting.

Economical Gilding.

The following is a good recipe for gilding common wares by dipping, or pot gilding : Cyanide of potassium 8 ozs., carbonate of potash 1 oz., cyanure of potassium 8 dwts., water 1 pint, chloride of gold 1 dwt. The mixture must be used at the boiling point, and after it has been applied, to be lasting, the gilt surfaces should be protected by varnishing.

Polishing Powder.

For cleaning some articles of jewellery, silver watch-cases, &c., a good powder may be prepared

L

by means of 4 parts of whiting and 1 part of rouge ; it can either be used dry, or mixed with alcohol or water. This mixture is easily brushed out of crevices, engraved work, or anything of a similar nature.

Gilding Steel.

Polished steel can be readily and beautifully gilded by using the ethereal solution of gold, which is thus prepared : Dissolve a small quantity of gold in *aqua-regia*, evaporate gently so as to drive off the superfluous acid, re-dissolve in water, and add three times its bulk of sulphuric ether. Allow to stand for twenty-four hours in a stoppered bottle, when the ethereal solution of gold will be found floating at the top. Polished steel dipped into this is at once gilded.

18-carat Gold.

To provide good workable 18-carat gold alloys, without flaws and cracks, which are found to present themselves in subsequent manipulations, much depends upon the first rolling of the bar. 18-carat should be subjected to a very heavy draught, the first and second time it is passed through the rolls. This imparts a grain to it close in texture, while light draughts stretch the gold on the surface and increase the coarseness of the grain, leaving the middle portion almost the same as when cast. This causes the gold, such as 18-carat, to crack and appear full of specks and flaws. Many good bars of 18-carat quality have been condemned and the fault laid to the melting, while it has been in the rolling all the time. We trust jewellers will act upon this hint.

To take Enamel out of Work.

Take powdered fluor spar, sufficient to well cover the article, mix into a thin liquid with oil of vitriol, and boil the article in the mixture, when the enamel will be removed. The fumes produced are injurious and should not be breathed.

Transparent Cement.

A good cement of the above description, for fastening any little thing in bezels, or settings, is made by dissolving $2\frac{1}{2}$ parts of clear gum arabic and 1 part of crystallized sugar in water; the mixture should be placed in a bottle, and put in a vessel of hot water until it assumes the consistency of syrup. It is then kept well corked until required for use.

Aluminum Silver.

Melt together copper 13 dwts., nickel 5 dwts., and aluminum 2 dwts.; this alloy is said to receive a high lustre and polish, and in many respects to imitate real silver of good quality.

Formula for Gilding like Polished Gold.

The following solution may be employed for gilding metal articles so as to look like polished gold by simply dipping them into the solution at a temperature of 130° to 150° Fahr.; the articles should be made perfectly bright before dipping. Dissolve 4 dwts. of fine gold in $\frac{3}{4}$ oz. of hydrochloric acid, and $\frac{1}{4}$ oz. of nitric acid; evaporate so as to expel as much of the acid as possible; dissolve in a pint of water and then throw down the gold by means of spirit of ammonia; well wash the precipitate. Next dissolve 2 ozs. of cyanide of potassium in just sufficient hot water to effect it, and dissolve the gold precipitate with this mixture. Filter the solution at this stage, and make up the solution to one quart by the addition of distilled water.

Formula for Silvering.

Dissolve 4 dwts. of fine silver in $\frac{1}{2}$ oz. of pure nitric acid, and ¼ oz. of water; precipitate the silver, to which you have added half a pint of water, with 4 dwts. of caustic soda dissolved in half a pint of water; well wash the precipitate with several fresh lots of hot water; then dissolve 1 oz. of cyanide of potassium in water, and dissolve the precipitate with it, and dilute with sufficient distilled water to make one quart of the mixture, and use in the same manner as the gilding solution.

To Solder Gold without changing its Colour.

Take of calcined borax 1 oz., sesquioxide of iron 1½ oz., ammonia ½ oz., mix with a little water to the consistency of cream, and apply to the surface of the article to be soldered, but not on the exact part to be joined together. Boil out in a pickle composed of oil of vitriol and water.

To boil Silver White.

Take cream of tartar 1 part, alum 1 part, salt 1 part, water 50 parts. Boil the work in this preparation until the desired whiteness is obtained. In common qualities it will be necessary to add some nitrate of silver to assist in its accomplishment.

18-carat Red Gold Alloy.

To prepare the above alloy take fine gold 1 oz., fine silver 16 grs., and refined copper 6 dwts., incorporate together by fusion in a plumbago crucible.

To Colour Gold a Deep Lemon Yellow.

The following mixture we have employed in colouring 15 and 18-carat gold alloys especially prepared for it :

Saltpetre . . .	4 ounces.
Common salt . .	2 ,,
Muriatic acid . .	1 ,,
Sulphuric acid . .	1 ,,
Water . . .	2 ,,
	10 ounces.

After having prepared the work it is dipped into the mixture at the boiling point for a period of three minutes, and then well sluiced in hot water, and returned to the colour-pot for one minute longer, and again well rinsed in fresh hot water. It is then ready for scratching or burnishing.

Yellow Metal for Gilding.

Take of copper 1 oz., zinc 4½ dwts., and tin 3 dwts., mix together by fusion in a clay crucible, and quench in water at a red heat. This alloy dips well and of a fine colour.

To give Gold a High and Fiery Colour.

Take of yellow brimstone 1 part, cream of tartar 1 part, and table salt (dried) 1 part, and mix together until they are in a state of fine powder. Then take as much as you can hold between the thumb and three fingers, and add it to as much water as would fill an ordinary glass. Boil the mixture and dip in the work for about six or eight seconds, and rinse well afterwards in clean water.

Gilders' Wax.

To produce a red colour on gilded, or for the matter of that, coloured work too, take of the fellowing ingredients and make into sticks for subsequent use :—

Yellow wax . . .	12 parts,
Verdigris . . .	4 ,,
Sulphate of zinc . .	4 ,,
Sulphate of iron . .	2 ,,
Bloodstone . . .	6 ,,
Copper scales . .	$2\frac{1}{2}$,,
Red oxide of iron .	$0\frac{1}{4}$,,
Borax	$0\frac{1}{4}$,,
	31 parts.

Melt the wax gradually and put in the other ingredients, which have previously been reduced to
powder and intimately well mixed together, stirring gently during the operation in order to produce one homogeneous mass, and prevent the
settling of the powder to the bottom of the vessel.
When cooled sufficient, form into sticks to be
afterwards employed. In using this composition
the articles to be coloured are slightly warmed, the
wax rubbed over them, then heated on a pan until
it is partly burnt off, cooled, and afterwards the
coating is dissolved by means of a weak pickle of
acid and water.

Yellow Gold Alloy to cost 40/ per oz.

Fine gold 9 dwts. 6 grs., fine silver 1 dwt.
15 grs., copper 6 dwts. 3 grs., pale composition
3 dwts., total 1 oz. This mixture produces an alloy
of a fine yellow tint, but it must on no account be
touched whilst hot or it will break to pieces.

Old-Fashioned Bright Gold Alloy.

The following is one of the old alloys of thirty
years ago, and was then extensively used for all
kinds of jewellery, more especially chains :—

	oz.	dwts.	grs
Fine gold . .	1	0	0
Fine silver . .	1	0	0
Pure copper . .	0	15	0
Composition . .	0	10	0
	3	5	0

It was about $7\frac{1}{2}$ carats, and the lowest alloy worked by respectable manufacturers. Its cost would be much more than the alloys of the present time equal in the fineness of the gold, consequent on the larger proportion of silver then employed to now. It was a good workable alloy, but nearly white in colour during the manipulations preceding the finished state.

CHAPTER XIV.

Collecting and Refining.

UNDER this heading we purpose describing the general mode of treatment adopted in jewellery establishments for the recovery of gold and silver which accumulates in different forms in the several workshops in accordance with the kind of work performed in each. It is known as *waste*, that being so because it cannot be collected and treated like ordinary *scrap*, but requires a special process to be adopted in order to bring it back again to the state required for working.

Ordinary scrap from gold and silver working requires no special treatment, other than that of simply melting like new material, to bring it again into working order. But the materials known as *lemel*; gilding, and colouring waste; scratch-brushing, polishing, and washing-out waste; becomes very impure by the accumulation of foreign

substances, and until these are removed or destroyed, it is a matter of impossibility to work
them, and for that reason these products are always
kept separate from all the substances which are
capable of being re-melted at any time without
special preparation.

In treating of these processes only those methods
will be given which have been proved economical
and of practical utility. We shall therefore commence with the collection of jewellers' lemel, which
consists of the filings, cuttings, turnings, and all
other dust-like particles which are detached from
the work in the course of manufacture. As each
workman has to look after, and is responsible for
the care of this waste until he weighs in his work,
the details of which are known to every workman
and master, it therefore calls for no description
here, further than that it should be weighed in as
free as possible from organic matter.

The lemel should be sieved through a fine sieve,
and only those particles preserved which are really
too fine to be melted in the ordinary manner, for
treatment by this process. The operation is performed by the free use of fluxes, and many have
been recommended for that purpose. Carbonate
of soda and ordinary washing soda have been
strongly urged and their advantages much dilated

on, by scientific men and teachers of technical
schools, consequent upon their cheapness; but there
is such a thing as a penny-wise and pound-foolish
policy sometimes engendered, and this can only be
proved by the test of long practical experience in
a subject to which it applies.

Ordinary washing soda is by far of too watery
a nature to be successfully and economically employed in lemel reduction, and its moistness in the
crucible is not in proportion, when assisted by
heat, to its original nature, becoming dry and more
difficult of quick fusion than some other salts to
which we intend to call attention. Carbonate, or
bi-carbonate of soda, is also devoid of that humidity
which should be the chief characteristic of a flux
for lemel reduction. Of all the fluxes there are
none more useful than *carbonate of potash*, and *bi-
carbonate of potash*, for reducing substances containing gold and silver in which organic matter is
present; or for filings, dust, or powder. Of either
of these it takes much less in quantity to perform
its work; does it more quickly and successfully;
acts less injuriously on the pots used for the operation; and at the same time becomes much more
liquescent ; and that more rapidly than the fluxes
above named.

Of course there are other fluxes possessed of

great merit that can be employed in the work we
are now speaking of, and some of these we shall,
by way of the following example, illustrate their
effectiveness, by showing the quantity of lemel a
given proportion is capable of reducing into a
metallic lump as being most essential to the present subject :—

FLUXES FOR LEMELS.

Salenixon	. .	8 ounces.
Common salt .	.	16 ,,
Lemel . .	.	200 ,,

The cost of this flux is 1d. and is quite effective
in collecting 200 ounces of lemel by using a large
clay crucible for holding the mixture. The flux
should be pounded into a fine powder, well mixed
with the lemel, and placed in the crucible, but not
within one inch of the top, as sometimes it rises
and may overflow if this precaution is not taken.

The salenixon is a good flux and prevents this
tendency to a very considerable extent, but it has
one disadvantage, it being liable to act somewhat
on the pot if the heat is continued too long, and
cause it to crack ; in that case it is always advisable
to keep by you, ready for use, some pounded bottle
glass, which can be added to the mass in the crucible
when any crack is perceived. This will make its

way to the crack in the pot and so prevent the
metal from running out and being lost in the fire.
This flux has been prepared by ourselves, and is of
general application to all the metals that are to be
met with in gold and silver manufacturing establishments.

It forces the gold and silver as it becomes fused
down to the bottom of the pot, and prevents ebul-
lition or boiling over of the mass; it forms a most
liquid flux, and by that means only a small
quantity is required in proportion to the lemel to
be reduced ; it does not become damp under atmo-
spheric influence ; and is, taken altogether, a most
powerful flux, as its power to reduce the above
fully proves. Here is another formula for collecting lemel :—

Brown American potash . 8 ounces.
Common salt . . . 4 ,,
Lemel . . . . . 100 ,,

The cost of this flux for reducing the above
quantity of lemel into a lump will be about 2d. It
is a most suitable flux for use when casting-pots
are employed. These pots before using should be
thoroughly well annealed, otherwise they will
crumble and fall to pieces.

Another formula we have used in experimenting

in this direction consisted of the following ingredients :—

Carbonate of soda	.	4 ounces.
Common salt .	. 2	,,
Salenixon .	. . 1	,,
Lemel .	. . 50	,,

It was not nearly so effective as either of the
previous mixtures, and required much more of the
flux to a given quantity of lemel to reduce the mass
to the humid state ; and also a more extensive and
longer continued heat to bring the lemel down,
from the causes previously pointed out in speaking
of soda as a flux at the commencement of this
chapter.

Here is another flux we have employed for the
same purpose, but it exhibited all the defects of
the last one, being much too dry in nature to ever
become popular in large manufactories, as a means
for collecting lemel :—

Washing soda .	.	3 ounces.
Argol .	. . 3	,,
Common salt .	. 3	,,
Lemel .	. . 50	,,

Sometimes it is found a very difficult matter
with dirty lemel to reduce the mass in the pot to a
liquid state, regardless of the flux employed. It is,

then, a good plan to add a small quantity of saltpetre occasionally to the mass, and this greatly
assists the fusion and brings down the filings, &c.,
when other means have failed; but care should be
taken not to add too much, or the pot will become
broken and the lemel spilled in the fire.

Plumbago crucibles may be employed for holding
the lemel while melting, and in that case very little
flux indeed should be used, as fluxes act on these
pots, and cause a dry, dirty mass to appear in the
pot from the action of the flux on the plumbago,
which becomes reduced in thickness, and this
refuse from the pot mixes with the lemel and
causes it to become almost infusible. Carbonate
of potash is the only flux that should be used in
such cases.

A very useful mixture for the collection of common stuff is made up of the following ingredients,
and when the lemel is intended to be sold as a
waste product to the refiner, it answers its purpose
admirably, its cost being next to nothing, whilst
its liquidness is great. The formula is :—

Soda ash .   .   .   4 ounces.
Common salt .   .   4   ,,
Rough lemel .   .   50   ,,

A large, ordinary clay crucible should be taken

and the lemel well mixed with the flux and then placed inside the crucible, and at once transferred to the furnace for melting. The lemel requires no previous burning, and if the pot is large enough no boiling over takes place; the melted lemel by its weight forces itself down to the bottom of the pot, from which it is recovered in a lump when the pot is cooled enough to be broken for that purpose.

The gilding and colouring waste requires a different flux to those above named, if the best means are utilised for their reduction into a lump of metal; as these waste products contain very much more foreign and organic substances to the worst samples of lemel, it is requisite that they should be dealt with accordingly. In the first place, if it is desired to know of the presence of gold and silver in a cyanide solution of either metal, it will only be necessary to ascertain this fact by placing in the solution a clean bright piece of zinc in the case of gold, and a clean bright piece of copper in the case of silver.

In a short time some of the gold will have become precipitated on the zinc, and some of the silver on the copper, either of which is readily enough distinguishable. There are several ways for recovering gold and silver from their solutions in cyanide of potassium, a brief reference to which

M

will now be made. The following is the *dry process:*—Heat the solution and evaporate the water by driving it off as steam, until a thick pasty mass only is left; dry this in a suitable pan, and mix the dry powder with the following flux, for reducing into a lump of metal.

Litharge .	.	.	4 ounces.
Soda ash .	.	.	8 ,,
Common salt	.	.	4 ,,
Gilding waste	.	.	50 ,,

Place this mixture in a fire-clay crucible and well fuse at a good heat; when the mass is reduced into quite liquid state, which is easily ascertained by stirring with a rod of iron, the pot is withdrawn from the fire, allowed to cool, and afterwards broken at the base, and the lump of mixed metals recovered for sale to the refiner, or placed aside for separate treatment for the recovery of the gold if so desired.

The colouring waste—which consists of the exhausted salts and rinsing waters—is placed in a large receptacle and diluted with water, the gold precipitated with copperas, the residue collected and dried in a cast-iron or other suitable vessel; the dried powder is then mixed with the above flux in about the same proportions, and fused until the metal has run in a lump to the bottom of the pot. The same treatment is then adopted as recommended for gilders' waste.

This flux produces a red-looking mixture and appears in strong contrast to those used for collecting lemel. It cannot be used when it is desired or intended to work up again the waste products, such, for instance, as lemel, on account of the lead in the litharge, which mixes with the other metals and destroys their workable qualities. The metal collected by this flux, when broken short, shows a dark fracture or grain.

For collecting lemel containing a variety of metals and intended for the refiner, it may be used with every advantage. It is a very suitable flux for collecting the gold from refuses, such as cyanide solutions, colour water sediment, dipping acid products, and all similar refuses which accumulate in the jeweller's workshop.

The following is the *wet process* for the recovery of gold from exhausted cyanide gilding solutions. The gold solution should be largely diluted with water, and then muriatic acid gradually poured in until no further effervescence takes place. The vessel containing the solution should be large, as the mixture rises when the acid is added and may boil over and thus lose a portion of the gold. The gas arising from the process is extremely poisonous, and the operation should therefore be performed in the open air. As old cyanide gilding solutions always contain mixed metals through all sorts of metals having been gilded therein, the precipitate will consist of the cyanides of gold and copper as well as chloride of silver.

The clear water above this precipitate is drawn off and put into the general waste-water tub, the precipitate well washed with hot water, then boiled in suitable quantities of *aqua regia*, which dissolves the gold and copper and leaves the chloride of silver as before in the same state. The solution containing the gold and copper is poured from the chloride of silver and either evaporated nearly to dryness in order to drive off excess of acid, or otherwise largely diluted with water and the gold precipitated into a metallic brown powder by means of the iron salt *copperas*. The copper is left behind in solution in its previous state. The gold has now only to be dried and melted by means of a suitable flux, and the result will be a lump of pure gold.

If preferred, after precipitating the mixed gold, silver, and copper, the sediment may be dried and the powder melted in the manner previously recommended by the dry process; but the resulting lump from that operation will be one of mixed metals, and not pure gold as in the case just described. Another method for collecting the gold from old gilding solutions is the following : Take a piece of platinum, or a plate of carbon, and con- nect it as an anode to the positive wire of the battery, and attach a piece of copper to the nega- tive wire, and suspend these in solution and pass a strong current through it until the gold has all become deposited on the copper. It may then either be used as an anode—if the gold is pure enough—or the gold dissolved off and recovered by the usual means.

The gold is recovered from *acid mixtures*, such as stripping, dead and bright pickling solutions, &c., by precipitation with *copperas*, added in excess. The acid mixture containing the gold should be diluted with water before the copperas is added. The precipitate is washed, dried, and then fused into a solid lump with carbonate of potash and a little saltpetre.

The silver is recovered from stripping acids and other pickling mixtures by diluting with water and then adding common salt or muriatic acid, either of which will throw down the dissolved silver in the form of chloride. This is collected, dried, and melted until it assumes the metallic state. The supernatant waters, as well as the rinsing waters from all these processes, should not be thrown away, but emptied into the general waste-water tub, as a further protection against the loss of any gold or silver which may have escaped recovery in any of these processes.

It is very seldom that these processes are required to be put in operation in the jeweller's workshop, as they do not pay for the cost of time and labour involved, regardless of the expense in providing the materials requisite for the purpose, nevertheless we give them for what they are worth. Probably the best and most economical plan would be to evaporate all excess of liquid by heat, and then mix the residues with the polishings, and sell to a refiner of jeweller's sweep. Acid mixtures should be evaporated in *acid proof* stoneware vessels, but alkaline mixtures can be reduced to a pasty mass in iron or cast-iron utensils manufactured for that purpose.

We have been often asked the question if it is possible to work up gold filings, little scraps of gold, and gold plated waste, &c. Now, as our view of the matter is to advance practical art by giving a comprehensive knowledge of the general and practical details of the alloying, working, and treating of gold and its useful compounds, by stating some of the results of our long experience, we gladly embrace the opportunity, more especially as the question has been asked and answered in several of the leading trading and scientific journals. Invariably the information imparted is not practical, or, in other words, such as could not be successfully applied in practice by the ordinary workman or jobbing jeweller to his pecuniary advantage, because it is imperfect in all practical details of mechanical art.

The *regime* of gold-working can only be adequately described by those who have actually played some practical part in it, and gained working knowledge by a display of experimental workshop manipulations. We claim to have had this experience, and as such, probably our remarks will be all the more welcomed by our readers.

Lead and soft solder are, amongst the metals, the most objectionable and the most likely to get mixed with jewellers' filings; especially will this be the case in a *jobber's* trade, from the repairing of articles containing portions of soft solder.

Now, in the re-melting of *gold* this solder is found most troublesome and difficult to deal with; and if this be the case with gold, how much more so must it be with filings or dust which contain impurities of all kinds. Contemporary works and trade journals have recommended the picking out of all impurities of a nature likely to prove injurious in the subsequent working of the prepared metal. This idea is at once preposterous to the practical working metallurgist, for all such-like feculent matter is too infinitesimal to be detected by the human eye; and as science has not yet discovered any mechanical contrivance in her deep researches to assist in and make the process an available one, we must adopt some other mode of treatment if we desire to be successful in the task of removing or destroying all extraneous matter with which dust or filings become impregnated. The best, most exact, and cheapest way to deal with substances of that kind is to well burn the filings in an iron ladle or some other equal substitute. This operation burns and destroys all organic matter, such as dirt, grease, and all other ingredients of a kindred nature, and thus brings the bulk down into a smaller compass. When this has cooled off a little the contents should be thoroughly magneted to remove therefrom every trace, if possible, of iron or steel filings, which are sure to get into the dust in the course of working the mother material. These extracted filings should be again preserved, and when a sufficient quantity has been accumulated, they may be sold to the *gold refiner*.

The gold dust should, after this operation, be put

into a fire-clay crucible—not plumbago—with the flux before recommended, and the top well covered with dried common salt, so as to protect the contents from the air and draught of the flues of the furnace. A good heat should be given of half an hour or so to enable the dust to become properly melted, to assist which a few crystals of saltpetre may be added towards the end of the operation to perfect the process. When the dust has become properly fused it will work its way to the bottom of the crucible. At this stage it should be withdrawn from the furnace and placed aside to cool in a secure place, and then the crucible may be broken at its base with a hammer, and the lump of gold will present itself in a form corresponding to the shape of the crucible.

As we have said before, the best and cheapest plan to deal with this kind of waste is to sell it to a gold refiner who has large appliances, and does his work on a large scale and consequently at the lowest possible cost, and he will either pay for the precious metals extracted in current coin or exchange the amount in new gold or silver, whichever is required. We may observe that no refiner will take an assay from the lump in its present form, therefore before submitting it for his test it will be absolutely necessary to again melt the

compound. This time it may be done in a plumbago pot with a little charcoal only as flux to protect it from the air, and when properly fused it
becomes a liquid, and may at once be removed
from the fire and poured into an ingot mould in
the same manner as an ordinary melting. The
previous lump of metal will now be in the form of
an ordinary bar, and in a perfect state for the
operation of the refiner.

Having now described the common and more
general method of treating the precious metal-
worker's lemel, we now go a step further by
entering into the details of a plan whereby all such
waste may be made to do duty again by its previous
operation, although we distinctly say that it is not
profitable with present prices for the small or large
manufacturer to undertake unless special advantages exist upon the premises for conducting the
process on a most economical scale; and as such
advantages seldom do exist, we are justified in
writing these remarks in opposition to the intro-
duction of the process by those persons less
experienced in jeweller's work, and whose labours
would be certain to result in ignominious failure.

The plan we intend now to speak of is called the
"Refining of Lemel," whereas the one already
described was simply the "Collecting of Lemel."

The former branch of the art is more chemical than the latter, and is always performed with an acid or acids which destroy the baser alloys from the more precious metal. Whenever this process is about to be performed, it will be necessary to first collect the lemel in the way already laid down, and then to ascertain its quality by means of the testing acid and needles. If the alloy is too good in quality it will not be so easily parted or separated from its baser ingredients by the acid which is to be subsequently introduced for its purification, therefore in the remelting it will be imperative that some extra alloy should be added to bring down the gold to the proper quality for parting; and as silver is the best metal to employ, enough of that material should be added so as to make the gold occupy the position of one-fourth part in the whole composition. This is to be added to the pot in the second melting process : and instead of pouring the contents of the crucible into an ingot mould it should be poured into a deep vessel of water from some height, in order to the more finely granulate the mixture; the molten mass must be very gradually poured in, or it will not be properly granulated, that is, reduced to fine grains ; stirring the water briskly in a circular direction greatly assists the operation of graining.

The mixture will now be found at the bottom of
the vessel in irregular grains or nuggets if the process has been well performed. These grains must
be carefully collected and dried and subsequently
placed in a glass flask free from lead—or any other
suitable vessel will do—and treated with acid.

The acid employed is that most corrosive one
known as *nitric acid* ; it may be used as follows,
and should always be in proportion to a given
weight of the material to be parted or purified. If
the nitric acid is of the best quality, and this is
necessary, it will be the safest to prepare the solution in these proportions :—

Alloy for parting .	.	1 ounce.
Pure nitric acid .	.	1 ,,
Water . . .	.	2 ,,

The mixture emits dangerous fumes, and great
care is required in the manipulation thereof to prevent danger to health. In the absence of proper
mechanical appliances, the process may be conducted upon a hearth, taking care that the fumes
escape effectually. Towards the end of the operation the fumes will begin to cease, partly because
the acid has done its work, and partly because
its action has been retarded by the amount of
work done ; therefore, before drawing off the

acid, it will be advisable to increase the temperature a little, in order to keep up the requisite chemical action and vigour.

In this way all the ingredients except the gold gradually become dissolved, and in order to perfectly complete the process, it will be absolutely necessary for a fresh supply of nitric acid to be added to the semi-dissolved mass, always removing the first one before an addition is made. By a repetition of these means the gold becomes pure and is in the form of a dark powder at the bottom of the operating vessel, and only required to be melted with a little flux, such as carbonate of potash, to show its true form and nature.

The undissolved gold at the bottom of the vessel should be well washed with hot water to remove all trace of acid previous to melting. If the gold has not been properly purified from its base ingredients it will not work properly, but be possessed of a brittleness most difficult to get rid of. To perform the process properly is more difficult than it appears to be. The nitric acid destroys the copper, silver, lead, tin, or pewter, with which the lemel may be contaminated, and, in fact, everything except the gold, always providing that the mixture has been properly prepared.

The silver in the acid is recovered by largely

diluting with water and precipitating with common salt or muriatic acid, which throws it down as chloride, in which state it is washed, dried, and melted. The copper can be precipitated by the immersion of a few pieces of iron in the solution withdrawn from the chloride of silver.

CHAPTER XV.

Sundry Gold Alloys.

THIS book would not be complete were we to omit from its pages a list of the gold alloys used in the various branches of the goldworker's trade for what may be justly termed special purposes, and as these mixtures are differently prepared to those used for regular purposes, we shall describe them as *Fancy Alloys*, so as to render them readily distinguishable from those in common use by giving a chapter to themselves.

18-CARAT PALE GOLD.

			oz.	dwts.	grs.
Fine gold	.	.	1	0	0
Fine silver	.	.	0	4	16
Pure copper	.	.	0	2	0
			1	6	16

Cost £3 4s. 9d. per oz.

18-CARAT FOR WATCH CASES.

			oz.	dwts.	grs.
Fine gold	.	.	1	0	0
Fine silver	.	.	0	4	0
Pure copper	.	.	0	2	16
			1	6	16

Cost £3 4s. 8d. per oz.

18-CARAT COLOURED GOLD.

			oz.	dwts.	grs.
Fine gold	.	.	1	0	0
Fine silver	.	.	0	3	8
Pure copper	.	.	0	3	8
			1	6	16

Cost £3 4s. 6d. per oz.

18-CARAT BURNISHING GOLD.

			oz.	dwts.	grs.
Fine gold	.	.	1	0	0
Fine silver	.	.	0	2	16
Pure copper	.	.	0	4	0
			1	6	16

Cost £3 4s. 5d. per oz.

18-CARAT RED GOLD.

			oz.	dwts.	grs.
Fine gold	.	.	1	0	0
Fine silver	.	.	0	1	8
Pure copper	.	.	0	5	8
			1	6	16

Cost £3 4s. 3d. per oz.

18-CARAT EXTRA RED GOLD.

	oz.	dwts.	grs.
Fine gold . .	I	o	o
Fine silver . .	o	o	16
Pure copper . .	o	6	o
	I	6	16

Cost £3 4s. 1d. per oz.

16-CARAT ALLOY SETTING GOLD.

	oz.	dwts.	grs.
Fine gold . .	I	o	o
Fine silver . .	o	6	o
Pure copper . .	o	4	o
	I	10	o

Cost £2 17s. 8d. per oz.

16-CARAT REGULAR GOLD.

	oz.	dwts.	grs.
Fine gold . .	I	o	o
Fine silver . .	o	3	9
Pure copper . .	o	6	15
	I	10	o

Cost £2 17s. 4d. per oz.

16-CARAT RED GOLD.

	oz.	dwts.	grs.
Fine gold . .	I	o	o
Fine silver . .	o	2	o
Pure copper . .	o	8	o
	I	10	o

Cost £2 17s. 2d. per oz.

N

15-CARAT YELLOW GOLD FOR POLISHING.

	oz.	dwts.	grs.
Fine gold . .	1	0	0
Fine silver . .	0	7	0
Pure copper . .	0	5	0
	1	12	0

Cost £2 14s. 3d. per oz.

15-CARAT COLOURED GOLD.

	oz.	dwts.	grs.
Fine gold . .	1	0	0
Fine silver . .	0	4	0
Pure copper . .	0	8	0
	1	12	0

Cost £2 13s. 10d. per oz.

15-CARAT RED GOLD.

	oz.	dwts.	grs.
Fine gold . .	1	0	0
Fine silver . .	0	2	12
Pure copper . .	0	9	12
	1	12	0

Cost £2 13s. 8d. per oz.

15-CARAT EXTRA RED GOLD.

	oz.	dwts.	grs.
Fine gold . .	1	0	0
Fine silver . .	0	1	6
Pure copper . .	0	10	18
	1	12	0

Cost £2 13s. 6d. per oz.

12-CARAT POLISHING GOLD.

			oz.	dwts.	grs.
Fine gold	.	.	1	0	0
Fine silver	.	.	0	12	0
Pure copper	.	.	0	8	0
			2	0	0

Cost £2 3s. 10d. per oz.

12-CARAT ORDINARY GOLD.

			oz.	dwts.	grs.
Fine gold	.	.	1	0	0
Fine silver	.	.	0	6	0
Pure copper	.	.	0	14	0
			2	0	0

Cost £2 3s. 4d. per oz.

12-CARAT RED GOLD.

			oz.	dwts.	grs.
Fine gold	.	.	1	0	0
Fine silver	.	.	0	2	12
Pure copper	.	.	0	17	12
			2	0	0

Cost £2 2s. 11d. per oz.

10-CARAT BRIGHT GOLD.

			oz.	dwts.	grs.
Fine gold	.	.	1	0	0
Fine silver	.	.	0	9	0
Pure copper	.	.	0	19	0
			2	8	0

Cost £1 16s. 4d. per oz.

9-CARAT ORDINARY GOLD.

	oz.	dwts.	grs.
Fine gold	1	0	0
Fine silver	0	8	0
Pure copper	1	5	8
	2	13	8

Cost £1 12s. 9d. per oz.

9-CARAT POLISHING GOLD.

	oz.	dwts.	grs.
Fine gold	1	0	0
Fine silver	0	13	8
Pure copper	1	0	0
	2	13	8

Cost £1 13s. 0d. per oz.

9-CARAT RED GOLD.

	oz.	dwts.	grs.
Fine gold	1	0	0
Fine silver	0	4	0
Pure copper	1	9	8
	2	13	8

Cost £1 12s. 4d. per oz.

8-CARAT BRIGHT GOLD FOR GILDING.

	oz	dwts.	grs.
Fine gold	1	0	0
Fine silver	0	7	0
Pure copper	1	13	0
	3	0	0

Cost £1 9s. 0d. per oz.

8-CARAT BRIGHT GOLD FOR POLISHING.

	oz.	dwts.	grs.
Fine gold . .	1	0	0
Fine silver . .	0	10	0
Pure copper . .	1	7	0
Composition . .	0	3	0
	3	0	0

Cost £1 9s. 2d. per oz.

7-CARAT BRIGHT GOLD FOR POLISHING.

	oz.	dwts.	grs.
Fine gold . .	1	0	0
Fine silver . .	0	15	0
Pure copper . .	1	10	12
Composition . .	0	3	0
	3	8	12

Cost £1 5s. 10d. per oz.

COMMON GOLD ALLOY FOR GILDING.

	oz.	dwts.	grs.
Fine gold . .	1	0	0
Fine silver . .	1	3	0
Pure copper . .	1	5	0
Composition .	0	4	0
	3	12	0

Cost £1 5s. 0d. per oz.

YELLOW GOLD FOR BRIGHT FINISHING.

	oz.	dwts.	grs.
Fine gold . .	1	0	0
Fine silver . .	0	7	0
Copper pure .	0	3	0
Composition . .	1	0	0
	2	10	0

Cost about £1 15s. 0d. per oz.

8-CARAT ACID RESISTING ALLOY.

	oz.	dwts.	grs.
Fine gold . .	1	0	0
Fine silver . .	1	5	0
Pure copper . .	0	15	0
	3	0	0

Cost £1 10s. 2d. per oz.

YANKEE GOLD ALLOY.

	oz.	dwts.	grs.
Fine gold . .	1	0	0
Fine silver . .	0	4	0
Pure copper . .	0	17	12
Pure spelter . .	0	1	12
	2	3	0

Cost £2 0s. 0d. per oz.

GOLD-PLATINUM ALLOY.

	oz.	dwts.	grs.
Fine gold . .	0	2	12
Platinum scrap .	0	5	0
Pure copper . .	0	10	0
Composition . .	0	2	12
	1	0	0

Cost £0 16s. 0d. per oz.

18-CARAT GOLD ALLOY FOR RINGS.

	oz.	dwts.	grs.
Fine gold . .	1	0	0
Fine silver . .	0	3	0
Pure copper .	0	3	16
	1	6	16

Cost £3 4s. 6d per oz.

9-CARAT ALLOY WITH GERMAN SILVER.

	oz.	dwts.	grs.
Fine gold . .	1	0	0
Best German silver .	0	8	0
Swedish copper wire	1	5	8
	2	13	8

Cost £1 12s. 1d. per oz.

15-CARAT GOLD ALLOY FOR RINGS.

	oz.	dwts.	grs.
Fine gold . .	1	0	0
Fine silver . .	0	4	0
Pure copper . .	0	8	0
	1	12	0

Cost £2 13s. 9d. per oz.

13 CARAT COLOURED ALLOY.

	oz.	dwts.	grs.
Fine gold . .	1	0	0
Fine silver . .	0	4	18
Copper wire . .	0	12	6
	1	17	0

Cost £2 6s. 9d. per oz.

14-CARAT ALLOY SAME COLOUR AS 18-CARAT.

	oz.	dwts.	grs.
Fine gold . .	1	0	0
Fine silver . .	0	2	12
Copper wire . .	0	9	0
Composition . .	0	2	18
	1	14	6

Cost £2 10s. 1d. per oz.

14-CARAT GOLD ALLOY WITHOUT SILVER.

	oz.	dwts.	grs.
Fine gold	1	0	0
Refined copper	0	12	6
Pure spelter	0	2	0
	1	14	6

Cost £2 9s. 10d. per oz.

FANCY COLOURED OR BRIGHT GOLD ALLOY.

	oz.	dwts.	grs.
Fine gold	1	0	0
Fine silver	0	5	0
Pure copper	0	8	8
	1	13	8

Cost £2 12s. 0d. per oz.

WET COLOURED GOLD SOLDER.

	oz.	dwts.	grs.
Four sovereigns	1	0	12
Fine silver	0	12	12
Copper wire	0	6	12
Composition	0	5	12
	2	5	0

Cost £1 16s. 9d. per oz.

BRIGHT GOLD SOLDER FOR RINGS.

	oz.	dwts.	grs.
Four sovereigns	1	0	12
Fine silver	1	1	0
Copper wire	0	13	12
	2	15	0

Cost £1 10s. 9d. per oz.

CURB SOLDER FOR 9-CARAT GOLD.

	oz.	dwts.	grs.
9-carat scrap	1	0	0
Fine silver	1	7	12
Pure copper	0	2	12
	2	10	0

Cost £0 15s. 0d. per oz.

KENSINGTON SOLDER FOR 9-CARAT GOLD.

	oz.	dwts.	grs.
9-carat scrap	1	0	0
Fine silver	0	14	0
Pure copper	0	1	0
	1	15	0

Cost £1 0s. 0d. per oz.

9-CARAT ALLOY FOR GOLD PINS.

	oz.	dwts.	grs.
Fine gold	1	0	0
Fine silver	0	5	0
Copper wire	1	3	8
Pure spelter	0	5	0
	2	13	8

Cost £1 12s. 6d. per oz.

20-CARAT GREEN GOLD ALLOY.

	oz.	dwts.	grs.
Fine gold	1	0	0
Fine silver	0	4	0
	1	4	0

Cost £3 11s. 9d. per oz.

16-CARAT RED GOLD FOR FANCY WORK.

	oz.	dwts.	grs.
Fine gold	1	0	0
Pure copper	0	10	0
	1	10	0

Cost £2 17s. 0d. per oz.

20-CARAT ENAMELLING GOLD ALLOY.

	oz.	dwts.	grs.
Fine gold	1	0	0
Fine silver	0	1	12
Pure copper	0	2	12
	1	4	0

Cost £3 11s. 6d. per oz.

12-CARAT TRANSPARENT ENAMELLING ALLOY.

	oz.	dwts.	grs.
Fine gold	1	0	0
Fine silver	0	14	0
Pure copper	0	6	0
	2	0	0

Cost £2 4s. 1d. per oz.

6-CARAT PALE GOLD ALLOY.

	oz.	dwts.	grs.
Fine gold	1	0	0
Fine silver	2	0	0
Pure copper	1	0	0
	4	0	0

Cost £1 3s. 6d. per oz.

EASY GOLD SOLDER FOR REPAIRING.

			oz.	dwts.	grs.
Gold alloy	.	.	1	0	0
Fine silver	.	.	0	5	0
Pure spelter	.	.	0	1	0
			1	6	0

Cost in proportion to quality of gold alloy.

PALE GOLD SOLDER, COLOURED.

			oz.	dwts.	grs.
18-carat scrap	.	.	1	0	0
Fine silver	.	.	0	16	0
			1	16	0

Cost £1 17s. 6d. per oz.

EASY COLOURED GOLD SOLDER.

			oz.	dwts.	grs.
Fine gold	.	.	0	8	0
Fine silver	.	.	0	7	6
Pure copper	.	.	0	4	0
Pure spelter	.	.	0	0	18
			1	0	0

Cost £1 15s. 6d. per oz.

DRY COLOURED GOLD SOLDER.

			oz.	dwts.	grs.
Fine gold	.	.	1	0	0
Fine silver	.	.	0	10	0
Pure spelter	.	.	0	2	0
			1	12	0

Cost £2 14s. 6d. per oz.

12½-CARAT GREEN GOLD ALLOY.

	oz.	dwts.	grs.
Four sovereigns .	1	0	12
Fine silver . .	0	13	0
Composition . .	0	2	12
	1	16	0

Cost £2 6s. 0d. per oz.

12½-CARAT RED GOLD ALLOY.

	oz.	dwts.	grs
Four sovereigns .	1	0	12
Fine silver . .	0	2	12
Pure copper . .	0	13	0
	1	16	0

Cost £2 4s. 9d. per oz.

12-CARAT COLOURED ALLOY.

	oz.	dwts.	grs.
Four sovereigns .	1	0	12
Fine silver . .	0	2	12
Pure copper . .	0	12	12
Composition . .	0	2	0
	1	17	12

Cost £2 3s. 0d. per oz.

H.M. SILVER ALLOY FOR WATCH CASES.

	oz.	dwts.	grs.
Fine silver . .	1	0	0
Nickel . . .	0	0	10
Copper . . .	0	0	20
Spelter . . .	0	0	10
	1	1	16

Cost £0 3s. 7d. per oz.

ANOTHER.

			oz.	dwts.	grs.
Fine silver	.	.	1	0	0
Best German	.	.	0	1	15
			1	1	15

Cost £0 3s. 7d. per oz.

H.M. SILVER ALLOY FOR STAMPINGS.

			oz.	dwts.	grs.
Fine silver	.	.	1	0	0
Nickel	.	.	0	1	0
Copper	.	.	0	0	15
			1	1	15

Cost £0 3s. 8d. per oz.

·800 SILVER ALLOY.

			oz.	dwts.	grs.
Fine silver	.	.	1	0	0
Best German	.	.	0	3	0
Copper	.	.	0	2	0
			1	5	0

Cost £0 3s. 4d. per oz.

·750 SILVER ALLOY.

			oz.	dwts.	grs.
Fine silver	.	.	1	0	0
Best German	.	.	0	5	0
Copper	.	.	0	1	16
			1	6	16

Cost £0 3s. 1d. per oz.

·500 SILVER ALLOY.

			oz.	dwts.	grs.
Fine silver	.	.	1	0	0
Best German	.	.	0	15	0
Copper	.	.	0	5	0
			2	0	0

Cost £0 2s. 1d. per oz.

HARD SILVER SOLDER.

			oz.	dwts.	grs.
Fine silver	.	.	1	0	0
Copper	.	.	0	5	0
			1	5	0

Cost £0 3s. 4d. per oz.

MEDIUM SILVER SOLDER.

			oz.	dwts.	grs.
Fine silver	.	.	1	0	0
Copper	.	.	0	5	0
Composition	.	.	0	5	0
			1	10	0

Cost £0 2s. 9d. per oz.

EASY SILVER SOLDER.

			oz.	dwts.	grs.
Fine silver	.	.	1	0	0
Composition	.	.	0	10	0
Pure spelter	.	.	0	5	0
			1	15	0

Cost £0 2s. 4d. per oz.

Pale Yellow Composition.

				oz.	dwts.	grs.
Copper	.	.	.	1	0	0
Spelter	.	.	.	0	10	0
				1	10	0

Deep Yellow Composition.

				oz.	dwts.	grs.
Copper	.	.	.	1	0	0
Spelter	.	.	.	0	6	16
				1	6	16

Auriferous Composition.

				oz.	dwts.	grs.
Copper	.	.	.	1	0	0
Spelter	.	.	.	0	5	0
				1	5	0

Another.

				oz.	dwts.	grs.
Copper	.	.	.	1	0	0
Spelter	.	.	.	0	4	0
				1	4	0

Gold-like Composition.

				oz.	dwts.	grs.
Copper	.	.	.	1	0	0
Spelter	.	.	.	0	2	21
				1	2	21

This composition can be used with or without silver in preparing the cheap 9-carat alloys now so much used for *Hall-marking purposes*. The whole of the alloys contained in this chapter have been verified by us, and can therefore thoroughly be depended upon as commercially sound and reliable for the purposes herein named. There are, of course, hundreds of others that could be given, but too much space would be occupied by further extension, and we presume enough has been said to explain and make the matter interesting to our readers from a scientific point of view, and also as showing the vast amount of skill and knowledge required in this department of the jeweller's business.

CHAPTER XVI.

Choice Recipes.

IN writing this book it has been our aim all through to give real and useful information of a practical nature, and before concluding we propose to relate some of the results of our experiments—which have been numerous—in the direction of better and more improved methods of practical skill being adopted in their relation to the modes of preparing, working, and finishing goldsmiths' work. These will take the form of an *abstract of research*, and as such will comprise many valuable secrets, as the following will show.

To Revive Coloured Gold Jewellery.

Take of the following ingredients :—Bi-carbonate of soda, 2 ozs.; chloride of lime, 1 oz., common salt, 1 oz.; boiling water, 8 ozs.; dip the work into this mixture at the boiling point for a short time, rinse, and wash in a warm solution of soap and water.

To Revive Silver Work.

When silver work has become tarnished by exposure in repeatedly exhibiting it before customers with a view to sale, it requires reviving occasionally to preserve a saleable condition. It can be improved by immersion in a mixture of borax and water, or in a strong solution of caustic soda at the point of boiling. In obstinate cases of tarnished goods dipping by means of zinc wires is more effective. After well brushing the work is much improved by the deft application of a little dry whiting.

Dipping Mixture for Watch Movements.

Nitric acid, 4 ozs.; sulphuric acid, 1 oz.; common salt, $\frac{1}{2}$ oz.; dissolve the salt in the sulphuric acid and then add the nitric acid. Dip while you count five, and immediately plunge into cold water to rinse away the acid which clings to the movements most tenaciously.

To Solder 18-carat Gold without Changing the Colour.

Take borax and calcine it, then of this take 1 oz.; of sesquioxide of iron, 1$\frac{1}{2}$ ozs.; spirits of ammonia,

½ oz.; mix with this into a paste and apply to the part about to be soldered, then boil out in sulphuric acid pickle and scratch-brush, when little difference will be perceived.

Solution for Deep Gilding.

Take of pure gold 2½ dwts.; of copper, 6 grs.; and of cyanide of potassium, 1½ ozs.; dissolve the gold in ½ oz. of nitro-muriatic acid, when thoroughly dissolved add the copper and dissolve into the gold mixture, then evaporate down until a red liquid of oily consistency shows itself. Dissolve the cyanide in a quart of hot water, and add to it the mixture of gold.

Deep Gold Anode for Gilding.

Take and incorporate together by melting :—Fine gold, 5 dwts.; pure copper, 12 grs.; cast, then roll into the shape and thickness required, and you have an anode capable of producing a high and rich colour.

A Mixture for Replenishing Gold Baths.

Chloride of gold, 1 part; cyanide of potassium, 1½ parts; water, 5 parts; keep in a well-stopperred bottle.

To Reduce 18-carat to 15-carat.

Take 18-carat scrap, 1 oz.; fine silver, 6 grs.; refined copper, 3 dwts. 18 grs.; total, 1 oz. 4 dwts.

Rich-looking Colour for Gold Work.

Boil after scratch-brushing from the process of colouring in the liquid *only* produced by that process for a few seconds, according to the pattern and design of the work.

Coloured Hollow Work.

After colouring, in order to perfectly neutralize the acid which clings inside the work and is not always removed by the rinsing waters, dip in a very dilute solution of ammonia; this prevents the action of the acid from taking effect and discolouring the work as it comes from the inside in drying. Crystals of soda will also do as well.

New Gold Alloy that may be coloured.

Take fine gold, 10 dwts.; fine silver, 18 grs.; pure copper, 7 dwts. 15 grs.; pale composition, 1 dwt. 15 grs.; total, 1 oz. Cost, £2 2s. 4d. per oz.

Yellow Metal for Dipping.

Copper, 1 oz.; grain tin, 3 dwts.; spelter, 4 dwts.; total, 1 oz. 7 dwts.

Metal for Gilding.

Copper, 1 oz.; spelter, 2 dwts.; total, 1 oz. 2 dwts.

Constant Battery for Gilding.

Take a stoneware jar 8 inches high and 6 inches in diameter, and a porous pot 9 inches high and 3 inches in diameter, outside measurements. Then procure 2 lbs. each of crushed carbon and peroxide of manganese, and a cylinder of carbon for the outer vessel and a rod of zinc for the porous vessel. When these have been provided, take the crushed carbon and manganese and mix well together, put them through a fine sieve in order to separate the fine dust; when this is done put them in the space between the two jars and around the carbon cylinder into within 1 inch of the top and fill up with melted pitch, inserting in the pitch before getting cold a small glass tube for allowing the gas and air to escape.

Inside the porous pot put the rod of zinc 1 inch longer than the porous pot, and fill with a solution of salammoniac in the proportion of $2\frac{1}{2}$ ozs. of salammoniac to the pint of water, and let stand for some hours; after that time the battery will be ready for use. This is a most suitable battery when only required at occasional intervals, as often is the case with manufacturing jewellers.

To Impart a Deep Colour to Gold.

Make a mixture of the following ingredients :—
Borax, 4 ozs. ; saltpetre, 2 ozs. ; common salt, 1 oz. ;
muriatic acid, 1 oz. ; old colouring liquid, 2 ozs. ;
total, 10 ozs.   Boil the work in this preparation for
three or four minutes, rinse and scratch-brush, and
a beautiful rich deep colour will be the result with
high quality gold alloys.

6-carat Alloy to stand Acid.

Gold coins, 1 oz. 12 grs. ; fine silver, 1 oz. 7 dwts.
12 grs. ; refined copper, 1 oz. 7 dwts. ; total, 3 ozs.
15 dwts.   This alloy is possessed of good workable
qualities, but rather pale in colour.

To Dissolve Copper.

Take chlorous acid, $\frac{1}{2}$ part ; muriatic acid, 2 parts ;
water, 20 parts.   Mix and put the copper therein.

New Colour for Red Gold Alloys.

Take saltpetre, 1 oz. ; glauber salt, 1 oz. ; muriatic
acid, 2 ozs. ; water, 6 ozs. ; total, 10 ozs.   Boil the
work in this mixture from three to five minutes
according to quality, and you will have a surpris-
ingly red colour like red gilding.

Composition for Niello Work.

Take of the following ingredients and treat according to instructions :—

Flowers of sulphur	.	12 ounces.
Pure lead .	. .	3½ ,,
Salammoniac .	.	2½ ,,
Pure copper .	.	2½ ,,
Fine silver	. .	0½ ,,

Make a paste of the sulphur with a little water, and put it into a crucible, melt the metals in another crucible with the salammoniac, and pour into the crucible which contains the sulphur. Calcine over the fire for some time, in fact until all the sulphurous vapour is driven off, then pulverise and make into a paste with salammoniac and water.

·250 Silver Alloy.

Fine silver, 1 oz.; best German silver, 2 ozs.; copper, 1 oz.; total, 4 ozs. This makes an excellent alloy of a good white colour.

Silver Solder for Steel.

Fine silver, 1 oz.; copper, 1 oz.; total, 2 ozs.

Old Gold Alloy.

Fine gold, 3 dwts.; fine silver, 1 dwt.; copper, 16 dwts.; total, 1 oz.

Arsenious Silver Alloy.

Copper, 9 dwts. 18 grs.; silver, 9 dwts. 18 grs.; arsenic, 12 grs.; total, 1 oz. Beautiful white colour.

French Silver Aluminum Alloy.

Fine silver, 6 dwts. 16 grs.; aluminum, 13 dwts. 8 grs.; total, 1 oz. This is one-third silver, and is said can be worked in every way to advantage. It is called *Tiers argent alloy.*

Black Gold Alloy.

Fine gold, 5 dwts.; fine silver, 15 dwts.; total, 1 oz. To produce the black colour it is only necessary to dip in the liquid produced from the colouring salts, or any oxidising mixture.

Gold Beaters' Gold.

Fine gold, 1 oz.; fine silver, 12 grs.; copper, 6 grs.; total, 1 oz. 18 grs.

To Remove Silver from Plated Articles.

Sulphuric acid, 8 ozs.; saltpetre, 1 oz. This mixture if kept free from water does not act on any other metal but silver. It should be used hot, when it will quickly strip plated articles of their silver.

A Deep Yellow Colour to Gold.

A method for producing a yellow tone to gold is as follows:—During the last dip in colouring add about a teaspoonful of finely powdered alum to the colouring salts. The same proportion of salammoniac will produce a rich deep orange tint if administered in the same way.

Watch Cases.

Silver watch-cases will not alloy with 18-carat gold under any conditions, as they contain spelter. Gold of 18-carat quality alloyed with them will break into pieces with the fingers when in the form of strips. Be careful, therefore, never to employ spelter in high quality gold alloys, as it renders them unfit for working.

Lemel.

Lemel reduced without common salt will not work properly. Therefore when it is intended to work up the gold again common salt should always be used, as saltpetre would destroy too much of the alloy.

Aluminum Solder.

Fine silver, 5 dwts. 18 grs.; grain tin, 5 dwts. 18 grs.; lead, 5 dwts. 18 grs.; zinc, 2 dwts. 18 grs.;

total, 1 oz. Melt the silver first, then add the tin,
afterwards the lead, and lastly the zinc, under cover
of fine charcoal powder to prevent the oxidising
influence of the air.

Platinum Solder.

It is the custom of the trade to solder platinum
when used alternately with gold with 18-carat gold,
and in some instances with 15-carat gold, but
nothing lower. But *pure silver* is the very best
solder that can be employed with platinum for all
such purposes, and this will be worth taking a note
of, as we have used it in our manufactory for years
for the work above-named.

8-carat Pale White Gold Alloy.

Fine gold, 6 dwts. 16 grs.; fine silver, 13 dwts.
8 grs.; total, 1 oz. This alloy is worked in the
same manner as any of the ordinary alloys, but will
not stand much heat in soldering, the fusible point
being very low.   It stands the acid test.

We shall now bring this treatise to a conclusion
by devoting a chapter to an accurately calculated
set of tables of mixed alloys, and trust to have
herein provided matter worthy of acceptance.

CHAPTER XVII.

Gold Values.

TABLE SHOWING THE RELATIVE VALUES OF THE DIFFERENT
CARATS OF FINE GOLD.

Carats.	Values.			Carats.	Values.		
	£	s.	d.		£	s.	d.
1	0	3	6½	13	2	6	0½
2	0	7	1	14	2	9	7
3	0	10	7½	15	2	13	1½
4	0	14	2	16	2	16	8
5	0	17	8½	17	3	0	2½
6	1	1	3	18	3	3	9
7	1	4	9½	19	3	7	3½
8	1	8	4	20	3	10	10
9	1	11	10½	21	3	14	4½
10	1	15	5	22	3	17	11
11	1	18	11½	23	4	1	5½
12	2	2	6	24	4	5	0

Gold Alloys.

TABLE SHOWING THE PROPORTIONS OF FINE GOLD TO BE
ADDED IN COMPOUNDING AN OUNCE OF ANY OF THE
FOLLOWING QUALITIES.

Quality.	Fine gold.			Alloy.			Total.		
Carat.	oz.	dwts.	grs.	oz.	dwts.	grs.	oz.	dwts.	grs.
1	0	0	20	0	19	4	1	0	0
2	0	1	16	0	18	8	1	0	0
3	0	2	12	0	17	12	1	0	0
4	0	3	8	0	16	16	1	0	0
5	0	4	4	0	15	20	1	0	0
6	0	5	0	0	15	0	1	0	0
7	0	5	20	0	14	4	1	0	0
8	0	6	16	0	13	8	1	0	0
9	0	7	12	0	12	12	1	0	0
10	0	8	8	0	11	16	1	0	0
11	0	9	4	0	10	20	1	0	0
12	0	10	0	0	10	0	1	0	0

Gold Alloys.

TABLE SHOWING THE PROPORTIONS OF FINE GOLD TO BE ADDED IN COMPOUNDING AN OUNCE OF ANY OF THE FOLLOWING QUALITIES.

Quality.	Fine gold.			Alloy.			Total.		
Carat.	oz.	dwts.	grs.	oz.	dwts.	grs.	oz.	dwts.	grs.
13	0	10	20	0	9	4	1	0	0
14	0	11	16	0	8	8	1	0	0
15	0	12	12	0	7	12	1	0	0
16	0	13	8	0	6	16	1	0	0
17	0	14	4	0	5	20	1	0	0
18	0	15	0	0	5	0	1	0	0
19	0	15	20	0	4	4	1	0	0
20	0	16	16	0	3	8	1	0	0
21	0	17	12	0	2	12	1	0	0
22	0	18	8	0	1	16	1	0	0
23	0	19	4	0	0	20	1	0	0
24	1	0	0		——		1	0	0

Gold Alloys.

TABLE SHOWING THE PROPORTIONS OF ALLOY TO BE ADDED TO ONE OUNCE OF FINE GOLD IN MAKING ANY OF THE FOLLOWING QUALITIES.

Quality.	Fine gold.			Alloy.			Total.		
Carat.	oz.	dwts.	grs.	oz.	dwts.	grs.	oz.	dwts.	grs.
1	1	0	0	23	0	0	24	0	0
2	1	0	0	11	0	0	12	0	0
3	1	0	0	7	0	0	8	0	0
4	1	0	0	5	0	0	6	0	0
5	1	0	0	3	16	0	4	16	0
6	1	0	0	3	0	0	4	0	0
7	1	0	0	2	8	12	3	8	12
8	1	0	0	2	0	0	3	0	0
9	1	0	0	1	13	8	2	13	8
10	1	0	0	1	8	0	2	8	0
11	1	0	0	1	3	15	2	3	15
12	1	0	0	1	0	0	2	0	0

Gold Alloys.

TABLE SHOWING THE PROPORTIONS OF ALLOY TO BE ADDED TO ONE OUNCE OF FINE GOLD IN MAKING ANY OF THE FOLLOWING QUALITIES.

Quality.	Fine gold.			Alloy.			Total.		
Carat.	oz.	dwts.	grs.	oz.	dwts.	grs.	oz.	dwts.	grs.
13	1	0	0	0	16	22	1	16	22
14	1	0	0	0	14	6	1	14	6
15	1	0	0	0	12	0	1	12	0
16	1	0	0	0	10	0	1	10	0
17	1	0	0	0	8	5	1	8	5
18	1	0	0	0	6	16	1	6	16
19	1	0	0	0	5	6	1	5	6
20	1	0	0	0	4	0	1	4	0
21	1	0	0	0	2	20	1	2	20
22	1	0	0	0	1	19	1	1	19
23	1	0	0	0	0	21	1	0	21
24	1	0	0	———			1	0	0

Gold Alloys.

TABLE SHOWING THE PROPORTIONS OF ALLOY TO BE ADDED TO 4 SOVEREIGNS (1 OZ. 12 GRS.) IN MAKING ANY OF THE FOLLOWING QUALITIES.

Quality.	Four sovereigns.			Alloy.			Total.		
Carat.	oz.	dwts.	grs.	oz.	dwts.	grs.	oz.	dwts.	grs.
1	1	0	12	21	9	12	22	10	0
2	1	0	12	10	4	12	11	5	0
3	1	0	12	6	9	12	7	10	0
4	1	0	12	4	12	0	5	12	12
5	1	0	12	3	9	12	4	10	0
6	1	0	12	2	14	12	3	15	0
7	1	0	12	2	4	0	3	4	12
8	1	0	12	1	15	18	2	16	6
9	1	0	12	1	9	12	2	10	0
10	1	0	12	1	4	12	2	5	0
11	1	0	12	1	0	12	2	1	0
12	1	0	12	0	17	0	1	17	12

Gold Alloys.

TABLE SHOWING THE PROPORTIONS OF ALLOY TO BE
ADDED TO 4 SOVEREIGNS (I OZ. I2 GRS.) IN MAKING
ANY OF THE FOLLOWING QUALITIES.

Quality.	Four sovereigns.			Alloy.			Total.		
Carat.	oz.	dwts.	grs.	oz.	dwts.	grs.	oz.	dwts.	grs.
13	1	0	12	0	14	6	1	14	18
14	1	0	12	0	11	18	1	12	6
15	1	0	12	0	9	12	1	10	0
16	1	0	12	0	7	15	1	8	3
17	1	0	12	0	6	0	1	6	12
18	1	0	12	0	4	12	1	5	0
19	1	0	12	0	3	4	1	3	16
20	1	0	12	0	2	0	1	2	12
21	1	0	12	0	1	0	1	1	12
22	1	0	12	Coins are made of this Quality.					
23	1	0	12	Better than Coins.					
24	1	0	12	Better than Coins.					

20-carat H.M. Alloys.

TABLE SHOWING THE PROPORTIONS OF ALLOY WITH FROM
I OZ. UP TO I3 OZS. OF FINE GOLD, AND CONTAINING
ABOUT I½ DWTS. OF FINE SILVER PER OZ.
COST 71/9 PER OZ.

Fine gold.	Fine silver.			Copper.			Total.		
oz.	oz.	dwts.	grs.	oz.	dwts.	grs.	oz.	dwts.	grs.
1	0	1	18	0	2	6	1	4	0
2	0	3	12	0	4	12	2	8	0
3	0	5	6	0	6	18	3	12	0
4	0	7	0	0	9	0	4	16	0
5	0	8	18	0	11	6	6	0	0
6	0	10	12	0	13	12	7	4	0
7	0	12	6	0	15	18	8	8	0
8	0	14	0	0	18	0	9	12	0
9	0	15	18	1	0	6	10	16	0
10	0	17	12	1	2	12	12	0	0
11	0	19	6	1	4	18	13	4	0
12	1	1	0	1	7	0	14	8	0
13	1	2	18	1	9	6	15	12	0

20-carat H.M. Alloys.

TABLE SHOWING THE PROPORTIONS OF ALLOY WITH FROM 4 UP TO 50 SOVEREIGNS, AND CONTAINING ABOUT 1¼ DWTS. OF FINE SILVER PER OZ. COST 71/6 PER OZ.

£	Gold coins.			Fine silver.			Copper.			Total.		
	oz.	dwts.	grs.	oz.	dwts.	grs.	oz.	dwts.	grs.	oz.	dwts.	grs.
4	1	0	12	0	1	12	0	0	12	1	2	12
8	2	1	0	0	3	0	0	1	0	2	5	0
12	3	1	12	0	4	12	0	1	12	3	7	12
16	4	2	0	0	6	0	0	2	0	4	10	0
20	5	2	12	0	7	12	0	2	12	5	12	12
24	6	3	0	0	9	0	0	3	0	6	15	0
28	7	3	12	0	10	12	0	3	12	7	17	12
32	8	4	0	0	12	0	0	4	0	9	0	0
36	9	4	12	0	13	12	0	4	12	10	2	12
40	10	5	0	0	15	0	0	5	0	11	5	0
44	11	5	12	0	16	12	0	5	12	12	7	12
48	12	6	0	0	18	0	0	6	0	13	10	0
50	12	16	6	0	18	18	0	6	6	14	1	6

18-carat H.M. Alloys.

TABLE SHOWING THE PROPORTIONS OF ALLOY WITH FROM 1 OZ. UP TO 13 OZS. OF FINE GOLD, AND CONTAINING ABOUT 1½ DWTS. OF FINE SILVER PER OZ. COST 64/6 PER OZ.

Fine gold.	Fine silver.			Copper.			Total.		
oz.	oz.	dwts.	grs.	oz.	dwts.	grs.	oz.	dwts.	grs.
1	0	2	0	0	4	16	1	6	16
2	0	4	0	0	9	8	2	13	8
3	0	6	0	0	14	0	4	0	0
4	0	8	0	0	18	16	5	6	16
5	0	10	0	1	3	8	6	13	8
6	0	12	0	1	8	0	8	0	0
7	0	14	0	1	12	16	9	6	16
8	0	16	0	1	17	8	10	13	8
9	0	18	0	2	2	0	12	0	0
10	1	0	0	2	6	16	13	6	16
11	1	2	0	2	11	8	14	13	8
12	1	4	0	2	16	0	16	0	0
13	1	6	0	3	0	16	17	6	16

18-carat H.M. Alloys.

TABLE SHOWING THE PROPORTIONS OF ALLOY WITH FROM
4 UP TO 50 SOVEREIGNS, AND CONTAINING ABOUT
1½ DWTS. OF FINE SILVER PER OZ.
COST 64/3 PER OZ.

£	Gold coins.			Fine silver.			Copper.			Total.		
	oz.	dwts.	grs.	oz.	dwts.	grs.	oz.	dwts.	grs.	oz.	dwts.	grs.
4	1	0	12	0	1	12	0	3	0	1	5	0
8	2	1	0	0	3	0	0	6	0	2	10	0
12	3	1	12	0	4	12	0	9	0	3	15	0
16	4	2	0	0	6	0	0	12	0	5	0	0
20	5	2	12	0	7	12	0	15	0	6	5	0
24	6	3	0	0	9	0	0	18	0	7	10	0
28	7	3	12	0	10	12	1	1	0	8	15	0
32	8	4	0	0	12	0	1	4	0	10	0	0
36	9	4	12	0	13	12	1	7	0	11	5	0
40	10	5	0	0	15	0	1	10	0	12	10	0
44	11	5	12	0	16	12	1	13	0	13	15	0
48	12	6	0	0	18	0	1	16	0	15	0	0
50	12	16	6	0	18	18	1	17	12	15	12	12

16-carat Coloured Alloys.

TABLE SHOWING THE PROPORTIONS OF ALLOY WITH FROM
1 OZ. UP TO 13 OZS. OF FINE GOLD, AND CONTAINING
ABOUT 1½ DWTS. OF FINE SILVER PER OZ.
COST 57/6 PER OZ.

Fine gold.	Fine silver.			Copper.			Total.		
oz.	oz.	dwts.	grs.	oz.	dwts.	grs.	oz.	dwts.	grs.
1	0	2	6	0	7	18	1	10	0
2	0	4	12	0	15	12	3	0	0
3	0	6	18	1	3	6	4	10	0
4	0	9	0	1	11	0	6	0	0
5	0	11	6	1	18	18	7	10	0
6	0	13	12	2	6	12	9	0	0
7	0	15	18	2	14	6	10	10	0
8	0	18	0	3	2	0	12	0	0
9	1	0	6	3	9	18	13	10	0
10	1	2	12	3	17	12	15	0	0
11	1	4	18	4	5	6	16	10	0
12	1	7	0	4	13	0	18	0	0
13	1	9	6	5	0	18	19	10	0

16-carat Gold Alloys.

TABLE SHOWING THE PROPORTIONS OF ALLOY WITH FROM 4 UP TO 50 SOVEREIGNS, AND CONTAINING ABOUT 1½ DWTS. OF FINE SILVER PER OZ.

COST 57/3 PER OZ.

£	Gold coins.			Fine silver.			Copper.			Total.		
	oz.	dwts.	grs.	oz.	dwts.	grs.	oz.	dwts.	grs.	oz.	dwts.	grs.
4	1	0	12	0	1	21	0	5	18	1	8	3
8	2	1	0	0	3	18	0	11	12	2	16	6
12	3	1	12	0	5	15	0	17	6	4	4	9
16	4	2	0	0	7	12	1	3	0	5	12	12
20	5	2	12	0	9	9	1	8	18	7	0	15
24	6	3	0	0	11	6	1	14	12	8	8	18
28	7	3	12	0	13	3	2	0	6	9	16	21
32	8	4	0	0	15	0	2	6	0	11	5	0
36	9	4	12	0	16	21	2	11	18	12	13	3
40	10	5	0	0	18	18	2	17	12	14	1	0
44	11	5	12	1	0	15	3	3	6	15	9	9
48	12	6	0	1	2	12	3	9	0	16	17	12
50	12	16	6	1	3	12	3	11	21	17	11	15

15-carat H.M. Alloys.

TABLE SHOWING THE PROPORTIONS OF ALLOY WITH FROM 1 OZ. UP TO 13 OZS. OF FINE GOLD, AND CONTAINING ABOUT 1½ DWTS. OF FINE SILVER PER OZ.

COST 54/ PER OZ.

Fine gold.	Fine silver.			Copper.			Total.		
oz.	oz.	dwts.	grs.	oz.	dwts.	grs.	oz.	dwts.	grs.
1	0	2	9	0	9	15	1	12	0
2	0	4	18	0	19	6	3	4	0
3	0	7	3	1	8	21	4	16	0
4	0	9	12	1	18	12	6	8	0
5	0	11	21	2	8	3	8	0	0
6	0	14	6	2	17	18	9	12	0
7	0	16	15	3	7	9	11	4	0
8	0	19	0	3	17	0	12	16	0
9	1	1	9	4	6	15	14	8	0
10	1	3	18	4	16	6	16	0	0
11	1	6	3	5	5	21	17	12	0
12	1	8	12	5	15	12	19	4	0
13	1	10	21	6	5	3	20	16	0

P

15-carat H.M. Alloys.

TABLE SHOWING THE PROPORTIONS OF ALLOY WITH FROM
4 UP TO 50 SOVEREIGNS, AND CONTAINING ABOUT
1½ DWTS. OF FINE SILVER PER OZ.

COST 53/9 PER OZ.

£	Gold coins.			Fine silver.			Copper.			Total.		
	oz.	dwts.	grs.	oz.	dwts.	grs.	oz.	dwts.	grs.	oz.	dwts.	grs.
4	1	0	12	0	2	0	0	7	12	1	10	0
8	2	1	0	0	4	0	0	15	0	3	0	0
12	3	1	12	0	6	0	1	2	12	4	10	0
16	4	2	0	0	8	0	1	10	0	6	0	0
20	5	2	12	0	10	0	1	17	12	7	10	0
24	6	3	0	0	12	0	2	5	0	9	0	0
28	7	3	12	0	14	0	2	12	12	10	10	0
32	8	4	0	0	16	0	3	0	0	12	0	0
36	9	4	12	0	18	0	3	7	12	13	10	0
40	10	5	0	1	0	0	3	15	0	15	0	0
44	11	5	12	1	2	0	4	2	12	16	10	0
48	12	6	0	1	4	0	4	10	0	18	0	0
50	12	16	6	1	5	0	4	13	18	18	15	0

14-carat Coloured Alloys.

TABLE SHOWING THE PROPORTIONS OF ALLOY WITH FROM
1 OZ. UP TO 13 OZS. OF FINE GOLD, AND CONTAINING
ABOUT 1½ DWTS. OF FINE SILVER PER OZ.

COST 50/3 PER OZ.

Fine gold.	Fine silver.			Copper.			Total.		
oz.	oz.	dwts.	grs.	oz.	dwts.	grs.	oz.	dwts.	grs.
1	0	2	12	0	11	18	1	14	6
2	0	5	0	1	2	12	3	8	12
3	0	7	12	1	15	6	5	2	18
4	0	10	0	2	7	0	6	15	0
5	0	12	12	2	18	18	8	11	6
6	0	15	0	3	10	12	10	5	12
7	0	17	12	4	2	6	11	19	18
8	1	0	0	4	14	0	13	14	0
9	1	2	12	5	5	18	15	8	6
10	1	5	0	5	17	12	17	2	12
11	1	7	12	6	9	6	18	16	18
12	1	10	0	7	1	0	20	11	0
13	1	12	12	7	12	18	22	5	6

14-carat Coloured Alloys.

TABLE SHOWING THE PROPORTIONS OF ALLOY WITH FROM 4 UP TO 50 SOVEREIGNS, AND CONTAINING ABOUT 1½ DWTS. OF FINE SILVER PER OZ.

COST 50/ PER OZ.

£	Gold coins.			Fine silver.			Copper.			Total.		
	oz.	dwts.	grs.	oz.	dwts.	grs.	oz.	dwts.	grs.	oz.	dwts.	grs.
4	1	0	12	0	2	6	0	9	12	1	12	6
8	2	1	0	0	4	12	0	19	0	3	4	12
12	3	1	12	0	6	18	1	8	12	4	16	18
16	4	2	0	0	9	0	1	18	0	6	9	0
20	5	2	12	0	11	6	2	7	12	8	1	6
24	6	3	0	0	13	12	2	17	0	9	13	12
28	7	3	12	0	15	18	3	6	12	11	5	18
32	8	4	0	0	18	0	3	16	0	12	18	0
36	9	4	12	1	0	6	4	5	12	14	10	6
40	10	5	0	1	2	12	4	15	0	16	2	12
44	11	5	12	1	4	18	5	4	12	17	14	18
48	12	6	0	1	7	0	5	14	0	19	7	0
50	12	16	6	1	8	3	5	18	18	20	3	3

Wet Coloured Alloys.

TABLE SHOWING THE PROPORTIONS OF ALLOY WITH FROM 1 OZ. UP TO 13 OZS. OF FINE GOLD, AND CONTAINING ABOUT 1½ DWTS. OF FINE SILVER PER OZ.

COST 45/6 PER OZ.

Fine gold.	Fine silver.			Copper.			Total.		
oz.	oz.	dwts.	grs.	oz.	dwts.	grs.	oz.	dwts.	grs.
1	0	2	18	0	15	6	1	18	0
2	0	5	12	1	10	12	3	16	0
3	0	8	6	2	5	18	5	14	0
4	0	11	0	3	1	0	7	12	0
5	0	13	18	3	16	6	9	10	0
6	0	16	12	4	11	12	11	8	0
7	0	19	6	5	6	18	13	6	0
8	1	2	0	6	2	0	15	4	0
9	1	4	18	6	17	6	17	2	0
10	1	7	12	7	12	12	19	0	0
11	1	10	6	8	7	18	20	18	0
12	1	13	0	9	3	0	22	16	0
13	1	15	18	9	18	6	24	14	0

Wet Coloured Alloys.

TABLE SHOWING THE PROPORTIONS OF ALLOY WITH FROM
4 UP TO 50 SOVEREIGNS, AND CONTAINING ABOUT
1½ DWTS. OF FINE SILVER PER OZ.

COST 45/ PER OZ.

£	Gold coins.			Fine silver.			Copper.			Total.		
	oz.	dwts.	grs.	oz.	dwts.	grs.	oz.	dwts.	grs.	oz.	dwts.	grs.
4	1	0	12	0	2	12	0	13	0	1	16	0
8	2	1	0	0	5	0	1	6	0	3	12	0
12	3	1	12	0	7	12	1	19	0	5	8	0
16	4	2	0	0	10	0	2	12	0	7	4	0
20	5	2	12	0	12	12	3	5	0	9	0	0
24	6	3	0	0	15	0	3	18	0	10	16	0
28	7	3	12	0	17	12	4	11	0	12	12	0
32	8	4	0	1	0	0	5	4	0	14	8	0
36	9	4	12	1	2	12	5	17	0	16	4	0
40	10	5	0	1	5	0	6	10	0	18	0	0
44	11	5	12	1	7	12	7	3	0	19	16	0
48	12	6	0	1	10	0	7	16	0	21	12	0
50	12	16	6	1	11	6	8	2	12	22	10	0

Wet Coloured Solder.

TABLE SHOWING THE PROPORTIONS OF ALLOY WITH FROM
1 OZ. UP TO 13 OZS. OF WET COLOURED SCRAP, AND
CONTAINING ABOUT 4¼ DWTS. OF FINE SILVER PER OZ.

COST 38/6 PER OZ.

Wet-Cold. Scrap.	Fine silver.			Spelter.			Total.		
oz.	oz.	dwts.	grs.	oz.	dwts.	grs.	oz.	dwts.	grs.
1	0	3	12	0	0	12	1	4	0
2	0	7	0	0	1	0	2	8	0
3	0	10	12	0	1	12	3	12	0
4	0	14	0	0	2	0	4	16	0
5	0	17	12	0	2	12	6	0	0
6	1	1	0	0	3	0	7	4	0
7	1	4	12	0	3	12	8	8	0
8	1	8	0	0	4	0	9	12	0
9	1	11	12	0	4	12	10	16	0
10	1	15	0	0	5	0	12	0	0
11	1	18	12	0	5	12	13	4	0
12	2	2	0	0	6	0	14	8	0
13	2	5	12	0	6	12	15	12	0

20-carat H.M. Reduced to 18-carat H.M.

TABLE SHOWING THE PROPORTIONS OF ALLOY WITH FROM
1 OZ. UP TO 13 OZS. OF 20-CARAT SCRAP, AND CONTAINING
ABOUT 1½ DWTS. OF FINE SILVER PER OZ.
COST 64/6 PER OZ.

20-c. H.m. Scrap.	Fine silver.			Copper.			Total.		
oz.	oz.	dwts.	grs.	oz.	dwts.	grs.	oz.	dwts.	grs.
1	0	0	3	0	2	0	1	2	3
2	0	0	6	0	4	0	2	4	6
3	0	0	9	0	6	0	3	6	9
4	0	0	12	0	8	0	4	8	12
5	0	0	15	0	10	0	5	10	15
6	0	0	18	0	12	0	6	12	18
7	0	0	21	0	14	0	7	14	21
8	0	1	0	0	16	0	8	17	0
9	0	1	3	0	18	0	9	19	3
10	0	1	6	1	0	0	11	1	6
11	0	1	9	1	2	0	12	3	9
12	0	1	12	1	4	0	13	5	12
13	0	1	15	1	6	0	14	7	15

20-carat H.M. Reduced to 16-carat H.M.

TABLE SHOWING THE PROPORTIONS OF ALLOY WITH FROM
1 OZ. UP TO 13 OZS. OF 20-CARAT SCRAP, AND CONTAINING
ABOUT 1½ DWTS. OF FINE SILVER PER OZ.
COST 57/6 PER OZ.

20-c. H.m. Scrap.	Fine silver.			Copper.			Total.		
oz.	oz.	dwts.	grs.	oz.	dwts.	grs.	oz.	dwts.	grs.
1	0	0	9	0	4	15	1	5	0
2	0	0	18	0	9	6	2	10	0
3	0	1	3	0	13	21	3	15	0
4	0	1	12	0	18	12	5	0	0
5	0	1	21	1	3	3	6	5	0
6	0	2	6	1	7	18	7	10	0
7	0	2	15	1	12	9	8	15	0
8	0	3	0	1	17	0	10	0	0
9	0	3	9	2	1	15	11	5	0
10	0	3	18	2	6	6	12	10	0
11	0	4	3	2	10	21	13	15	0
12	0	4	12	2	15	12	15	0	0
13	0	4	21	3	0	3	16	5	0

20-carat H.M. Reduced to 15-carat H.M.

TABLE SHOWING THE PROPORTIONS OF ALLOY WITH FROM
I OZ. UP TO I3 OZS. OF 20-CARAT SCRAP, AND CONTAINING
ABOUT I½ DWTS. OF FINE SILVER PER OZ.

COST 53/9 PER OZ.

20-c. H.m. Scrap.	Fine silver.			Copper.			Total.		
oz.	oz.	dwts.	grs.	oz.	dwts.	grs.	oz.	dwts.	grs.
I	0	0	12	0	6	4	I	6	16
2	0	I	0	0	12	8	2	13	8
3	0	I	12	0	18	12	4	0	0
4	0	2	0	I	4	16	5	6	16
5	0	2	12	I	10	20	6	13	8
6	0	3	0	I	17	0	8	0	0
7	0	3	12	2	3	4	9	6	16
8	0	4	0	2	9	8	10	13	8
9	0	4	12	2	15	12	12	0	0
10	0	5	0	3	I	16	13	6	16
II	0	5	12	3	7	20	14	13	8
12	0	6	0	3	14	0	16	0	0
13	0	6	12	4	0	4	17	6	16

20-carat H.M. Reduced to 14-carat H.M.

TABLE SHOWING THE PROPORTIONS OF ALLOY WITH FROM
I OZ. UP TO I3 OZ. OF 20-CARAT SCRAP, AND CONTAINING
ABOUT I½ DWTS. OF FINE SILVER PER OZ.

COST 50/ PER OZ.

20-c. H.m. Scrap.	Fine silver.			Copper.			Total.		
oz.	oz.	dwts.	grs.	oz.	dwts.	grs.	oz.	dwts.	grs.
I	0	0	15	0	8	3	I	8	18
2	0	I	6	0	16	6	2	17	12
3	0	I	21	I	4	9	3	6	6
4	0	2	12	I	12	12	5	15	0
5	0	3	3	2	0	15	7	3	18
6	0	3	18	2	8	18	8	12	12
7	0	4	9	2	16	21	10	I	6
8	0	5	0	3	5	0	11	10	0
9	0	5	15	3	13	3	12	18	18
10	0	6	6	4	I	6	14	7	12
II	0	6	21	4	9	9	15	16	6
12	0	7	12	4	17	12	17	5	0
13	0	8	3	5	5	15	18	13	18

20-carat H.M. Reduced to 12½-carat.

TABLE SHOWING THE PROPORTIONS OF ALLOY WITH FROM
I OZ. UP TO 13 OZS. OF 20-CARAT SCRAP, AND CONTAINING
ABOUT 1½ DWTS. OF FINE SILVER PER OZ.
COST 45/ PER OZ.

20-c. H.m. Scrap.	Fine silver.			Copper.			Total.		
oz.	oz.	dwts.	grs.	oz.	dwts.	grs.	oz.	dwts.	grs.
1	0	1	0	0	11	0	1	12	0
2	0	2	0	1	2	0	3	4	0
3	0	3	0	1	13	0	4	16	0
4	0	4	0	2	4	0	6	8	0
5	0	5	0	2	15	0	8	0	0
6	0	6	0	3	6	0	9	12	0
7	0	7	0	3	17	0	11	4	0
8	0	8	0	4	8	0	12	16	0
9	0	9	0	4	19	0	14	8	0
10	0	10	0	5	10	0	16	0	0
11	0	11	0	6	1	0	17	12	0
12	0	12	0	6	12	0	19	4	0
13	0	13	0	7	3	0	20	16	0

18-carat H.M. Reduced to 16-carat.

TABLE SHOWING THE PROPORTIONS OF ALLOY WITH FROM
I OZ. UP TO 13 OZS. OF 18-CARAT SCRAP, AND CONTAINING
ABOUT 1½ DWTS. OF FINE SILVER PER OZ.
COST 57/6 PER OZ.

18-c. H.m. Scrap.	Fine silver.			Copper.			Total.		
oz.	oz.	dwts.	grs.	oz.	dwts.	grs.	oz.	dwts.	grs.
1	0	0	4	0	2	8	1	2	12
2	0	0	8	0	4	16	2	5	0
3	0	0	12	0	7	0	3	7	12
4	0	0	16	0	9	8	4	10	0
5	0	0	20	0	11	16	5	12	12
6	0	1	0	0	14	0	6	15	0
7	0	1	4	0	16	8	7	17	12
8	0	1	8	0	18	16	8	0	0
9	0	1	12	1	1	0	9	2	12
10	0	1	16	1	3	8	10	5	0
11	0	1	20	1	5	16	11	7	12
12	0	2	0	1	8	0	12	10	0
13	0	2	4	1	10	8	13	12	12

18-carat H.M. Reduced to 15-carat H.M.

TABLE SHOWING THE PROPORTIONS OF ALLOY WITH FROM
1 OZ. UP TO 13 OZS. OF 18-CARAT SCRAP, AND CONTAINING
ABOUT 1½ DWTS. OF FINE SILVER PER OZ.

COST 53/9 PER OZ.

18-c. H.m. Scrap.	Fine silver.			Copper.			Total.		
oz.	oz.	dwts.	grs.	oz.	dwts.	grs.	oz.	dwts.	grs.
1	0	0	6	0	3	18	1	4	0
2	0	0	12	0	7	12	2	8	0
3	0	0	18	0	11	6	3	12	0
4	0	1	0	0	15	0	4	16	0
5	0	1	6	0	18	18	6	0	0
6	0	1	12	1	2	12	7	4	0
7	0	1	18	1	6	6	8	8	0
8	0	2	0	1	10	0	9	12	0
9	0	2	6	1	13	18	10	16	0
10	0	2	12	1	17	12	12	0	0
11	0	2	18	2	1	6	13	4	0
12	0	3	0	2	5	0	14	8	0
13	0	3	6	2	8	18	15	12	0

18-carat H.M. Reduced to 14-carat.

TABLE SHOWING THE PROPORTIONS OF ALLOY WITH FROM
1 OZ. TO 13 OZS. OF 18-CARAT SCRAP, AND CONTAINING
ABOUT 1½ DWTS. OF FINE SILVER PER OZ.

COST 50/ PER OZ.

18-c. H.m. Scrap.	Fine silver.			Copper.			Total.		
oz.	oz.	dwts.	grs.	oz.	dwts.	grs.	oz.	dwts.	grs.
1	0	0	9	0	5	9	1	5	18
2	0	0	18	0	10	18	2	11	12
3	0	1	3	0	16	3	3	17	6
4	0	1	12	1	1	12	5	3	0
5	0	1	21	1	6	21	6	8	18
6	0	2	6	1	12	6	7	14	12
7	0	2	15	1	17	15	9	0	6
8	0	3	0	2	3	0	10	6	0
9	0	3	9	2	8	9	11	11	18
10	0	3	18	2	13	18	12	17	12
11	0	4	3	2	19	3	14	3	6
12	0	4	12	3	4	12	15	9	0
13	0	4	21	3	9	21	16	14	18

18-carat H.M. Reduced to 12½-carat.

TABLE SHOWING THE PROPORTIONS OF ALLOY WITH FROM
1 OZ. UP TO 13 OZS. OF 18-CARAT SCRAP, AND CONTAINING
ABOUT 1½ DWTS. OF FINE SILVER PER OZ.
COST 4 5/ PER OZ.

18-c. H.m. Scrap.	Fine silver.			Copper.			Total.		
oz.	oz.	dwts.	grs.	oz.	dwts.	grs.	oz.	dwts.	grs.
1	0	0	18	0	8	0	1	8	18
2	0	1	12	0	16	0	2	17	12
3	0	2	6	1	4	0	4	6	6
4	0	3	0	1	12	0	5	15	0
5	0	3	18	2	0	0	7	3	18
6	0	4	12	2	8	0	8	12	12
7	0	5	6	2	16	0	10	1	6
8	0	6	0	3	4	0	11	10	0
9	0	6	18	3	12	0	12	18	18
10	0	7	12	4	0	0	14	7	12
11	0	8	6	4	8	0	15	16	6
12	0	9	0	4	16	0	17	5	0
13	0	9	18	5	4	0	18	13	18

16-carat Reduced to 15-carat H.M.

TABLE SHOWING THE PROPORTIONS OF ALLOY WITH FROM
1 OZ. UP TO 13 OZS. OF 16-CARAT SCRAP, AND CONTAINING
ABOUT 1½ DWTS. OF FINE SILVER PER OZ.
COST 54/ PER OZ.

16-carat Scrap.	Fine silver.			Copper.			Total.		
oz.	oz.	dwts.	grs.	oz.	dwts.	grs.	oz.	dwts.	grs.
1	0	0	3	0	1	3	1	1	6
2	0	0	6	0	2	6	2	2	12
3	0	0	9	0	3	9	3	3	18
4	0	0	12	0	4	12	4	5	0
5	0	0	15	0	5	15	5	6	6
6	0	0	18	0	6	18	6	7	12
7	0	0	21	0	7	21	7	8	18
8	0	1	0	0	9	0	8	10	0
9	0	1	3	0	10	3	9	11	6
10	0	1	6	0	11	6	10	12	12
11	0	1	9	0	12	9	11	13	18
12	0	1	12	0	13	12	12	15	0
13	0	1	15	0	14	15	13	16	6

16-carat Reduced to 14-carat.

TABLE SHOWING THE PROPORTIONS OF ALLOY WITH FROM
1 OZ. UP TO 13 OZS. OF 16-CARAT SCRAP, AND CONTAINING
ABOUT 1½ DWTS. OF FINE SILVER PER OZ.

COST 50/ PER OZ.

16-carat Scrap.	Fine silver.			Copper.			Total.		
oz.	oz.	dwts.	grs.	oz.	dwts.	grs.	oz.	dwts.	grs.
1	0	0	6	0	2	18	1	3	0
2	0	0	12	0	5	12	2	6	0
3	0	0	18	0	8	6	3	9	0
4	0	1	0	0	11	0	4	12	0
5	0	1	6	0	13	18	5	15	0
6	0	1	12	0	16	12	6	18	0
7	0	1	18	0	19	6	8	1	0
8	0	2	0	1	2	0	9	4	0
9	0	2	6	1	4	18	10	7	0
10	0	2	12	1	7	12	11	10	0
11	0	2	18	1	10	6	12	13	0
12	0	3	0	1	13	0	13	16	0
13	0	3	6	1	15	18	14	19	0

16-carat Reduced to 12½-carat.

TABLE SHOWING THE PROPORTIONS OF ALLOY WITH FROM
1 OZ. UP TO 13 OZS. OF 16-CARAT SCRAP, AND CONTAINING
ABOUT 1½ DWTS. OF FINE SILVER PER OZ.

COST 45/ PER OZ.

16-carat Scrap.	Fine silver.			Copper.			Total.		
oz.	oz.	dwts.	grs.	oz.	dwts.	grs.	oz.	dwts.	grs.
1	0	0	9	0	5	6	1	5	15
2	0	0	18	0	10	12	2	11	6
3	0	1	3	0	15	18	3	16	21
4	0	1	12	1	1	0	5	2	12
5	0	1	21	1	6	6	7	8	3
6	0	2	6	1	11	12	8	13	18
7	0	2	15	1	16	18	9	19	9
8	0	3	0	2	2	0	10	5	0
9	0	3	9	2	7	6	11	10	15
10	0	3	18	2	12	12	12	16	6
11	0	4	3	2	17	18	14	1	21
12	0	4	12	3	3	0	15	7	12
13	0	4	21	3	8	6	16	13	3

15-carat H.M. Reduced to 14-carat.

TABLE SHOWING THE PROPORTIONS OF ALLOY WITH FROM I OZ. UP TO 13 OZS. OF 15-CARAT SCRAP, AND CONTAINING ABOUT 1½ DWTS. OF FINE SILVER PER OZ.

COST 50/ PER OZ.

15-c. H.m. Scrap.	Fine silver.			Copper.			Total.		
oz.	oz.	dwts.	grs.	oz.	dwts.	grs.	oz.	dwts.	grs.
1	0	0	3	0	1	9	1	1	12
2	0	0	6	0	2	18	2	3	0
3	0	0	9	0	4	3	3	4	12
4	0	0	12	0	5	12	4	6	0
5	0	0	15	0	6	21	5	7	1..
6	0	0	18	0	8	6	6	9	0
7	0	0	21	0	9	15	7	10	12
8	0	1	0	0	11	0	8	12	0
9	0	1	3	0	12	9	9	13	12
10	0	1	6	0	13	18	10	15	0
11	0	1	9	0	15	3	11	16	12
12	0	1	12	0	16	12	12	18	0
13	0	1	15	0	17	21	13	19	12

15-carat H.M. Reduced to Wet-Coloured.

TABLE SHOWING THE PROPORTIONS OF ALLOY WITH FROM I OZ. UP TO 13 OZS. OF 15-CARAT SCRAP, AND CONTAINING ABOUT 1½ DWTS. OF FINE SILVER PER OZ.

COST 45/ PER OZ.

15-c. H.m. Scrap.	Fine silver.			Copper.			Total.		
oz.	oz.	dwts.	grs.	oz.	dwts.	grs.	oz.	dwts.	grs.
1	0	0	6	0	3	18	1	4	0
2	0	0	12	0	7	12	2	8	0
3	0	0	18	0	11	6	3	12	0
4	0	1	0	0	15	0	4	16	0
5	0	1	6	0	18	18	6	0	0
6	0	1	12	1	2	12	7	4	0
7	0	1	18	1	6	6	8	8	0
8	0	2	0	1	10	0	9	12	0
9	0	2	6	1	13	18	10	16	0
10	0	2	12	1	17	12	12	0	0
11	0	2	18	2	1	6	13	4	0
12	0	3	0	2	5	0	14	8	0
13	0	3	6	2	8	18	15	12	0

14-carat Reduced to 12½-carat.

TABLE SHOWING THE PROPORTIONS OF ALLOY WITH FROM
1 OZ. UP TO 13 OZS. OF 14-CARAT SCRAP, AND CONTAINING
ABOUT 1½ DWTS. OF FINE SILVER PER OZ.

COST 45/ PER OZ.

14-carat Scrap.	Fine silver.			Copper.			Total.		
oz.	oz.	dwts.	grs.	oz.	dwts.	grs.	oz.	dwts.	grs.
1	0	0	4	0	2	2	1	2	6
2	0	0	8	0	4	4	2	4	12
3	0	0	12	0	6	6	3	6	18
4	0	0	16	0	8	8	4	9	0
5	0	0	20	0	10	10	5	11	6
6	0	1	0	0	12	12	6	13	12
7	0	1	4	0	14	14	7	15	18
8	0	1	8	0	16	16	8	18	0
9	0	1	12	0	18	18	10	0	6
10	0	1	16	1	0	20	11	2	12
11	0	1	20	1	2	22	12	4	18
12	0	2	0	1	5	0	13	7	0
13	0	2	4	1	7	2	14	9	6

12-carat H.M. Alloys.

TABLE SHOWING THE PROPORTIONS OF ALLOY WITH FROM
1 OZ. UP TO 13 OZS. OF FINE GOLD, AND CONTAINING
ABOUT 2 DWTS. OF FINE SILVER PER OZ.

COST 43/6 PER OZ.

Fine gold.	Fine silver.			Copper.			Total.		
oz.	oz.	dwts.	grs.	oz.	dwts.	grs.	oz.	dwts.	grs.
1	0	4	0	0	16	0	2	0	0
2	0	8	0	1	12	0	4	0	0
3	0	12	0	2	8	0	6	0	0
4	0	16	0	3	4	0	8	0	0
5	1	0	0	4	0	0	10	0	0
6	1	4	0	4	16	0	12	0	0
7	1	8	0	5	12	0	14	0	0
8	1	12	0	6	8	0	16	0	0
9	1	16	0	7	4	0	18	0	0
10	2	0	0	8	0	0	20	0	0
11	2	4	0	8	16	0	22	0	0
12	2	8	0	9	12	0	24	0	0
13	2	12	0	10	8	0	26	0	0

12-carat H.M. Alloys.

TABLE SHOWING THE PROPORTIONS OF ALLOY WITH FROM
4 UP TO 50 SOVEREIGNS, AND CONTAINING ABOUT 2
DWTS. OF FINE SILVER PER OZ.

COST 43/3 PER OZ.

£	Gold coins.			Fine silver.			Copper.			Total.		
	oz.	dwts.	grs.	oz.	dwts.	grs.	oz.	dwts.	grs.	oz.	dwts.	grs.
4	1	0	12	0	3	12	0	13	12	1	17	12
8	2	1	0	0	7	0	1	7	0	3	15	0
12	3	1	12	0	10	12	2	0	12	5	12	12
16	4	2	0	0	14	0	2	14	0	7	10	0
20	5	2	12	0	17	12	3	7	12	9	7	12
24	6	3	0	1	1	0	4	1	0	11	5	0
28	7	3	12	1	4	12	4	14	12	13	2	12
32	8	4	0	1	8	0	5	8	0	15	0	0
36	9	4	12	1	11	12	6	1	12	16	17	12
40	10	5	0	1	15	0	6	15	0	18	15	0
44	11	5	12	1	18	12	7	8	12	20	12	12
48	12	6	0	2	2	0	8	2	0	22	10	0
50	12	16	6	2	3	18	8	8	18	23	8	18

10-carat Full Alloys.

TABLE SHOWING THE PROPORTIONS OF ALLOY WITH FROM
1 OZ. UP TO 13 OZS. OF FINE GOLD, AND CONTAINING
ABOUT 2¼ DWTS. OF FINE SILVER PER OZ.

COST 36/6 PER OZ.

Fine gold.	Fine silver.			Copper.			Total.		
oz.	oz.	dwts.	grs.	oz.	dwts.	grs.	oz.	dwts.	grs.
1	0	5	12	1	2	12	2	8	0
2	0	11	0	2	5	0	4	16	0
3	0	16	12	3	7	12	7	4	0
4	1	2	0	4	10	0	9	12	0
5	1	7	12	5	12	12	12	0	0
6	1	13	0	6	15	0	14	8	0
7	1	18	12	7	17	12	16	16	0
8	2	4	0	9	0	0	19	4	0
9	2	9	12	10	2	12	21	12	0
10	2	15	0	11	5	0	24	0	0
11	3	0	12	12	7	12	26	8	0
12	3	6	0	13	10	0	28	16	0
13	3	11	12	14	12	12	31	4	0

10-carat Full Alloys.

TABLE SHOWING THE PROPORTIONS OF ALLOY WITH FROM 4 UP TO 50 SOVEREIGNS, AND CONTAINING ABOUT $2\frac{1}{4}$ DWTS. OF FINE SILVER PER OZ.

COST 36/3 PER OZ.

£	Gold coins.			Fine silver.			Copper.			Total.		
	oz.	dwts.	grs.	oz.	dwts.	grs.	oz.	dwts.	grs.	oz.	dwts.	grs.
4	1	0	12	0	4	18	0	19	18	2	5	0
8	2	1	0	0	9	12	1	19	12	4	10	0
12	3	1	12	0	14	6	2	19	6	6	15	0
16	4	2	0	0	19	0	3	19	0	9	0	0
20	5	2	12	1	3	18	4	18	18	11	5	0
24	6	3	0	1	8	12	5	18	12	13	10	0
28	7	3	12	1	13	6	6	18	6	15	15	0
32	8	4	0	1	18	0	7	18	0	18	0	0
36	9	4	12	2	2	18	8	17	18	20	5	0
40	10	5	0	2	7	12	9	17	12	22	10	0
44	11	5	12	2	12	6	10	17	6	24	15	0
48	12	6	0	2	17	0	11	17	0	27	0	0
50	12	16	6	2	19	9	12	6	21	28	2	12

9-carat H.M. Alloys.

TABLE SHOWING THE PROPORTIONS OF ALLOY WITH FROM 1 OZ. UP TO 13 OZS. OF FINE GOLD, AND CONTAINING ABOUT $2\frac{1}{2}$ DWTS. OF FINE SILVER PER OZ.

COST 33/ PER OZ.

Fine gold.	Fine silver.			Copper.			Total.		
oz.	oz.	dwts.	grs.	oz.	dwts.	grs.	oz.	dwts.	grs.
1	0	6	16	1	6	16	2	13	8
2	0	13	8	2	13	8	5	6	16
3	1	0	0	4	0	0	8	0	0
4	1	6	16	5	6	16	10	13	8
5	1	13	8	6	13	8	13	6	16
6	2	0	0	8	0	0	16	0	0
7	2	6	16	9	6	16	18	13	8
8	2	13	8	10	13	8	21	6	16
9	3	0	0	12	0	0	24	0	0
10	3	6	16	13	6	16	26	13	8
11	3	13	8	14	13	8	29	6	16
12	4	0	0	16	0	0	32	0	0
13	4	6	16	17	6	16	34	13	8

9-carat H.M. Alloys.

TABLE SHOWING THE PROPORTIONS OF ALLOY WITH FROM 4 UP TO 50 SOVEREIGNS, AND CONTAINING ABOUT 2½ DWTS. OF FINE SILVER PER OZ.

COST 32/9 PER OZ.

£	Gold coins.			Fine silver.			Copper.			Total.		
	oz.	dwts.	grs.	oz.	dwts.	grs.	oz.	dwts.	grs.	oz.	dwts.	grs.
4	1	0	12	0	6	0	1	3	12	2	10	0
8	2	1	0	0	12	0	2	7	0	5	0	0
12	3	1	12	0	18	0	3	10	12	7	10	0
16	4	2	0	1	4	0	4	14	0	10	0	0
20	5	2	12	1	10	0	5	17	12	12	10	0
24	6	3	0	1	16	0	7	1	0	15	0	0
28	7	3	12	2	2	0	8	4	12	17	10	0
32	8	4	0	2	8	0	9	8	0	20	0	0
36	9	4	12	2	14	0	10	11	12	22	10	0
40	10	5	0	3	0	0	11	15	0	25	0	0
44	11	5	12	3	6	0	12	18	12	27	10	0
48	12	6	0	3	12	0	14	2	0	30	0	0
50	12	16	12	3	15	0	14	13	18	31	5	0

9-carat Regular Alloys.

TABLE SHOWING THE PROPORTIONS OF ALLOY WITH FROM 1 OZ. UP TO 13 OZS. OF FINE GOLD, AND CONTAINING ABOUT 3 DWTS. OF FINE SILVER PER OZ.

COST 31/ PER OZ.

Fine gold.	Fine silver.			Copper.			Total.		
oz.	oz.	dwts.	grs.	oz.	dwts.	grs.	oz.	dwts.	grs.
1	0	8	12	1	8	6	2	16	18
2	0	17	0	2	16	12	5	13	12
3	1	5	12	4	4	18	8	10	6
4	1	14	0	5	13	0	11	7	0
5	2	2	12	7	1	6	14	3	18
6	2	11	0	8	9	12	17	0	12
7	2	19	12	9	17	18	19	17	6
8	3	8	0	11	6	0	22	14	0
9	3	16	12	12	14	6	25	10	18
10	4	5	0	14	2	12	28	7	12
11	4	13	12	15	10	18	31	4	6
12	5	2	0	16	19	0	34	1	0
13	5	10	12	18	7	6	36	17	18

9-carat Regular Alloys.

TABLE SHOWING THE PROPORTIONS OF ALLOY WITH FROM
4 UP TO 50 SOVEREIGNS, AND CONTAINING ABOUT 3
DWTS. OF FINE SILVER PER OZ.

COST 30/9 PER OZ.

£	Gold coins.			Fine silver.			Copper.			Total.		
	oz.	dwts.	grs.	oz.	dwts.	grs.	oz.	dwts.	grs.	oz.	dwts.	grs.
4	1	0	12	0	7	12	1	5	12	2	13	12
8	2	1	0	0	15	0	2	11	0	5	7	0
12	3	1	12	1	2	12	3	16	12	8	0	12
16	4	2	0	1	10	0	5	2	0	10	14	0
20	5	2	12	1	17	12	6	7	12	13	7	12
24	6	3	0	2	5	0	7	13	0	16	1	0
28	7	3	12	2	12	12	8	18	12	18	14	12
32	8	4	0	3	0	0	10	4	0	21	8	0
36	9	4	12	3	7	12	11	9	12	24	1	12
40	10	5	0	3	15	0	12	15	0	26	15	0
44	11	5	12	4	2	12	14	0	12	29	8	12
48	12	6	0	4	10	0	15	6	0	32	2	0
50	12	16	6	4	13	18	15	18	18	33	8	18

Bright Gold Solder.

TABLE SHOWING THE PROPORTIONS OF ALLOY WITH FROM
1 OZ. UP TO 13 OZS. OF FINE GOLD, AND CONTAINING
ABOUT 6 DWTS. OF FINE SILVER PER OZ.

COST 30/ PER OZ.

Fine gold.	Fine silver.			Composition.			Total.		
oz.	oz.	dwts.	grs.	oz.	dwts.	grs.	oz.	dwts.	grs.
1	0	18	0	1	2	0	3	0	0
2	1	16	0	2	4	0	6	0	0
3	2	14	0	3	6	0	9	0	0
4	3	12	0	4	8	0	12	0	0
5	4	10	0	5	10	0	15	0	0
6	5	8	0	6	12	0	18	0	0
7	6	6	0	7	14	0	21	0	0
8	7	4	0	8	16	0	24	0	0
9	8	2	0	9	18	0	27	0	0
10	9	0	0	11	0	0	30	0	0
11	9	18	0	12	2	0	33	0	0
12	10	16	0	13	4	0	36	0	0
13	11	14	0	14	6	0	39	0	0

12-carat H.M. Reduced to 10-carat.

TABLE SHOWING THE PROPORTIONS OF ALLOY WITH FROM I OZ. UP TO 13 OZS. OF 12-CARAT SCRAP, AND CONTAINING ABOUT 2¼ DWTS. OF FINE SILVER PER OZ.

COST 36/6 PER OZ.

12-carat Scrap.	Fine silver.			Copper.			Total.		
oz.	oz.	dwts.	grs.	oz.	dwts.	grs.	oz.	dwts.	grs.
1	0	0	16	0	3	8	1	4	0
2	0	1	8	0	6	16	2	8	0
3	0	2	0	0	10	0	3	12	0
4	0	2	16	0	13	8	4	16	0
5	0	3	8	0	16	16	6	0	0
6	0	4	0	1	0	0	7	4	0
7	0	4	16	1	3	8	8	8	0
8	0	5	8	1	6	16	9	12	0
9	0	6	0	1	10	0	10	16	0
10	0	6	16	1	13	8	12	0	0
11	0	7	8	1	16	16	13	4	0
12	0	8	0	2	0	0	14	8	0
13	0	8	16	2	3	8	15	12	0

12-carat H.M. Alloys Reduced to 9-carat H.M.

TABLE SHOWING THE PROPORTIONS OF ALLOY WITH FROM I OZ. UP TO 13 OZS. OF 12-CARAT SCRAP, AND CONTAINING ABOUT 2½ DWTS. OF FINE SILVER PER OZ.

COST 33/ PER OZ.

12-carat Scrap.	Fine silver.			Copper.			Total.		
oz.	oz.	dwts.	grs.	oz.	dwts.	grs.	oz.	dwts.	grs.
1	0	1	9	0	5	3	1	6	12
2	0	2	18	0	10	6	2	13	0
3	0	4	3	0	15	9	3	19	12
4	0	5	12	1	0	12	5	6	0
5	0	6	21	1	5	15	6	12	12
6	0	8	6	1	10	18	7	19	0
7	0	9	15	1	15	21	9	5	12
8	0	11	0	2	1	0	10	12	0
9	0	12	9	2	6	3	11	18	12
10	0	13	18	2	11	6	13	5	0
11	0	15	3	2	16	9	14	11	12
12	0	16	12	3	1	12	15	18	0
13	0	17	21	3	6	15	17	4	12

12-carat H.M. Reduced to 9-carat Regular.

TABLE SHOWING THE PROPORTIONS OF ALLOY WITH FROM
1 OZ. UP TO 13 OZS. OF 12-CARAT SCRAP, AND CONTAIN-
ING ABOUT 3 DWTS. OF FINE SILVER PER OZ.
COST 31/ PER OZ.

12-carat Scrap.	Fine silver.			Copper.			Total.		
oz.	oz.	dwts.	grs.	oz.	dwts.	grs.	oz.	dwts.	grs.
1	0	2	6	0	6	6	1	8	12
2	0	4	12	0	12	12	2	17	0
3	0	6	18	0	18	18	4	5	12
4	0	9	0	1	5	0	5	14	0
5	0	11	6	1	11	6	7	2	12
6	0	13	12	1	17	12	8	11	0
7	0	15	18	2	3	18	9	19	12
8	0	18	0	2	10	0	11	8	0
9	1	0	6	2	16	6	12	16	12
10	1	2	12	3	2	12	14	5	0
11	1	4	18	3	8	18	15	13	12
12	1	7	0	3	15	0	17	2	0
13	1	9	6	4	1	6	18	10	12

10-carat Reduced to 9-carat H.M.

TABLE SHOWING THE PROPORTIONS OF ALLOY WITH FROM
1 OZ. UP TO 13 OZS. OF 10-CARAT SCRAP, AND CONTAIN-
ING ABOUT $2\frac{1}{2}$ DWTS. OF FINE SILVER PER OZ.
COST 33/ PER OZ.

10-carat Scrap.	Fine silver.			Copper.			Total.		
oz.	oz.	dwts.	grs.	oz.	dwts.	grs.	oz.	dwts.	grs.
1	0	0	12	0	1	15	1	2	3
2	0	1	0	0	3	6	2	4	6
3	0	1	12	0	4	21	3	6	9
4	0	2	0	0	6	12	4	8	12
5	0	2	12	0	8	3	5	10	15
6	0	3	0	0	9	18	6	12	18
7	0	3	12	0	11	9	7	14	21
8	0	4	0	0	13	0	8	17	0
9	0	4	12	0	14	15	9	19	3
10	0	5	0	0	16	6	11	1	6
11	0	5	12	0	17	21	12	3	9
12	0	6	0	0	19	12	13	5	12
13	0	6	12	1	1	3	14	7	15

10-carat Reduced to 9-carat Regular.

TABLE SHOWING THE PROPORTIONS OF ALLOY WITH FROM
1 OZ. UP TO 13 OZS. OF 10-CARAT SCRAP, AND CONTAIN-
ING ABOUT 3 DWTS. OF FINE SILVER PER OZ.

COST 31/ PER OZ.

10-carat Scrap.	Fine silver.			Copper.			Total.		
oz.	oz.	dwts.	grs.	oz.	dwts.	grs.	oz.	dwts.	grs.
1	0	1	6	0	2	18	1	4	0
2	0	2	12	0	5	12	2	8	0
3	0	3	18	0	8	6	3	12	0
4	0	5	0	0	11	0	4	16	0
5	0	6	6	0	13	18	6	0	0
6	0	7	12	0	16	12	7	4	0
7	0	8	18	0	19	6	8	8	0
8	0	10	0	1	2	0	9	12	0
9	0	11	6	1	4	18	10	16	0
10	0	12	12	1	7	12	12	0	0
11	0	13	18	1	10	6	13	4	0
12	0	15	0	1	13	0	14	8	0
13	0	16	6	1	15	18	15	12	0

9-carat H.M. Reduced to 9-carat Regular.

TABLE SHOWING THE PROPORTIONS OF ALLOY WITH FROM
1 OZ. UP TO 13 OZS. OF 9-CARAT H. M. SCRAP, AND
CONTAINING ABOUT 3 DWTS. OF FINE SILVER PER OZ.

COST 31/ PER OZ.

9-c. H.m. Scrap.	Fine silver.			Copper.			Total.		
oz.	oz.	dwts.	grs.	oz.	dwts.	grs.	oz.	dwts.	grs.
1	0	0	18	0	0	18	1	1	12
2	0	1	12	0	1	12	2	3	0
3	0	2	6	0	2	6	3	4	12
4	0	3	0	0	3	0	4	6	0
5	0	3	18	0	3	18	5	7	12
6	0	4	12	0	4	12	6	9	0
7	0	5	6	0	5	6	7	10	12
8	0	6	0	0	6	0	8	12	0
9	0	6	18	0	6	18	9	13	12
10	0	7	12	0	7	12	10	15	0
11	0	8	6	0	8	6	11	16	12
12	0	9	0	0	9	0	12	18	0
13	0	9	18	0	9	18	13	19	12

GOLD VALUES.

Decimal Tables.

TABLE SHOWING THE CONVERSION OF PENNYWEIGHTS
AND GRAINS INTO DECIMALS OF AN OUNCE.

Grains.	Ounces.	Pennyweights.	Ounces.
½	·001	1	·05
1	·002	2	·10
2	·004	3	·15
3	·006	4	·20
4	·008	5	·25
5	·010	6	·30
6	·012	7	·35
7	·015	8	·40
8	·017	9	·45
9	·019	10	·50
10	·021	11	·55
11	·023	12	·60
12	·025	13	·65
13	·027	14	·70
14	·029	15	·75
15	·031	16	·80
16	·033	17	·85
17	·035	18	·90
18	·037	19	·95
19	·040	20	1·00
20	·042		
21	·044		
22	·046		
23	·048		
24	·050		

INDEX.

THE END.

PRINTED BY J. S. VIRTUE AND CO., LIMITED, CITY ROAD, LONDON.